THE
DELICIOUS WORLD
OF
RAW FOODS

THE
DELICIOUS WORLD
OF
RAW FOODS

A Culinary Guide to Preparing Appetizers,
Soups, Salads, Vegetables, Main Dishes,
and Desserts with Little or No Cooking

BY

MARY LOUISE LAU

Rawson Associates Publishers, Inc.

New York

The quotation from T.S. Eliot's
"Little Gidding," in FOUR QUARTERS,
© copyright 1943 by T.S. Eliot,
renewed 1971 by Esne Valery Eliot,
is reprinted by permission of
Harcourt Brace Jovanovich, Inc.

The quotation from James Houston's
"The White Dawn," © copyright 1971
by James Houston, is reprinted by permission
of Harcourt Brace Jovanovich, Inc.

Illustrated by Kathryn Wirch

Library of Congress Cataloging in Publication Data

Lau, Mary Louise.
    The delicious world of raw foods.
    Includes index.
    1.   Cookery.   2.   Food, Raw.   I.   Title.
TX652.L36   1977   641.5   76-50513
ISBN 0-89256-011-8
ISBN 0-89256-068-1 pbk.

Published simultaneously in Canada by
McClelland and Stewart, Ltd.
Manufactured in the United States of America
by American Book—Stratford Press
Saddle Brook, New Jersey
First Paperback Edition

Rawson Associates Publishers, Inc.
630 Third Avenue
New York, New York 10017

To Graham, Adam,
Dad, Veida and, above all,
Wesley

ACKNOWLEDGMENTS

VERY SPECIAL THANKS go to those who were readers of early and later drafts of this book, and generous with recipes, advice and good wishes all along the way: Veronica McLaughlin, Cynthia Lawrence, Gail Cottingham, Sharon Barovsky, Joan Burns, Kay Berger, Ralph Pinkerton of the California Avocado Advisory Board, Virginia and Edmund Gilbert, Marcie Barkin, Helen Gurley Brown, Fran Hansford, Veida Morrow Metcalf, James Metcalf and Wesley Lau. Special thanks to Gladys Emerson of U.C.L.A. for reviewing some sections. And to Essie Wyrick, who shared many explorations with me.

Many more thanks to Joan White, Betty Parker, Ike and Mitsouko Royer, Lynn Freeman, Joe Maross, Carolyn Zimmer, Norman Rossington, Jo Morrow, Agnes Lau, Marilyn Galanoy, Marjorie Bowen, Mary Carmichael Snyder, Michel of Scandia, John Dougherty, Larry and Leanna Heath, Veida Marie Corbett, Kirsten Rumar, Phyllis Sokol, Lillian Glick, Ed Meyer, Judy and Don Bistany, Harold Leventhal, Bob Haddad, Andrea Giambrone and to all of the many friends, acquaintances and business associates who contributed raw food recipes and expertise. Among the many restaurants whose imaginative and traditional ways with raw food dishes inspired me: Scandia, Perino's, Au Petit Cafe, Studio Grill, Hotel Ritz, Madrid, Senor Pico, Oso Sushi,

Yamato, and countless regional restaurants of the United States, Italy, Mexico, and Spain.

Warmest gratitude is reserved for those professionals who have made this book possible: Knox Burger, my formidable agent; Reid Miles, who superbly arranged and photographed the foods on the cover; Kathryn Wirch, whose distinguished drawings illustrate the book, and Carolyn Anthony, my gifted and tactful editor. And loving gratitude to my mother, Margaret Stiles Metcalf, who taught me to appreciate the elegance, and the importance of fresh, quality source foods.

Research sources, too numerous to list here, are gratefully acknowledged. They would include at least a thousand fascinating books on food and cooking, dating from pre-history down through the Roman Empire to present times, with emphasis on 19th and 20th century food and cooking. Raw food traditions abound in every region of the world, so many of the sources are international.

Finally, the ultimate acknowledgment: the raw foods themselves. They are their own tradition, a cuisine unto themselves. It has been a wonder and a pleasure to move among them as an historian, a reporter, and simply a happy eater. Hopefully, this book will be a welcome, often-used addition to your kitchen, and an inviting introduction to this most natural and perfect of cuisines, The Delicious World of Raw Foods.

MARY LOUISE LAU
Los Angeles, June 1977

CONTENTS

We shall not cease from exploration and the end of all our exploring will be to arrive where we started and know the place for the first time.

T. S. ELIOT

THE
DELICIOUS WORLD
OF
RAW FOODS

1. GOOD THINGS TO KNOW ABOUT RAW FOODS

THERE IS NO GOURMET RECIPE, no inspired blending of spices, no masking or processing, no industrial magic that can match the taste of fresh, choice foods in the raw, just as nature made them.

Cooking can be fun, of course, and necessary. Its warm, sizzling pleasures are not to be denied, and its practical values are inestimable.

But the best, total perfection, is the raw food itself, eaten at its peak of freshness. The juicy, ripe, sweet meat of a perfect peach. The tender, indescribably satisfying sensation of rare filet mignon. The crisp, tingling-cool bite of a gently bred cucumber. The savory, chewy zap of fresh pecans or premium black walnuts, unearthed from their pretty shells. The mouthwatering joy of a freshly picked, sun-warmed strawberry. The shocking sweetness of a truly fresh sweet young pea, just popped out of its silky cradle.

The list is endless. And so is the delicious world of raw foods. With a mere handful of exceptions, virtually all the foods we eat are wholesome and delicious in their natural, very fresh state. Nature does the cooking for us.

The indispensable trademark of any great restaurant anywhere in the world is a fanatic devotion to the freshest, most select of foods. The quest is richly rewarded. Caviar is flown with precise care from the rivers of Russia to everywhere in the world. Fine Hawaiian tuna is flown hourly from Japan, with the most delicate of handling, to the sashimi tables of the world. World-famous chefs often guard their prime local fresh-food sources with zealous pride. And every distinguished menu boasts a group of deftly procured, elegantly prepared raw-food dishes. For the ultimate wisdom of the greatest and most talented cooks is knowing when *not* to cook, when not to tamper with nature's perfection.

So why are we cooking so many foods that should be eaten raw? Why are we slaving away when a delicious gourmet raw-food life is often so much simpler?

Cooking is an old habit, a throwback to the days when there was no refrigerated shipping, and when, come October, most fresh foods disappeared from the market. Canning, preserving, cooking, pickling, smoking, and brining became not only the way to survive, but appetizing ways to eat.

Now all that has changed. Skilled agriculture, modern shipping, and sophisticated distribution have made the delicious world of raw foods a happy reality for all of us for most months of the year. And it is more than just delicious gourmet eating, for it has astonishing advantages that make it even more appealing as part of our contemporary lifestyle. Here are a few things you should know:

The world of raw foods is luxurious but economical. If cooking "from scratch" with fresh ingredients is a notorious money-saver, *not* cooking saves even more money. You don't pay for packaging or processing. You don't pay for precooking. You often buy foods in season, when their prices are lowest. And you buy the exact quantities you want. If the foods are local, you don't pay for shipping.

If you're price-conscious, the ultimate economies of eating raw foods are positively breathtaking. Not one penny is wasted on junk food, or on nutrition losses through cooking (which usually average 25 percent), or in food shrinkage through cooking (up to 50 percent and more on some foods), or on loss of the flavorful natural moisture in fresh foods.

Raw foods are always more nutritious. It's a beautiful, effortless way to shed your nutritional worries. Books have been written about, doctors have proven, and nutritionists sing the praises of the superior nutritive values of raw food. But all you need to know is one simple fact: *No food is ever improved nutritionally by cooking.* Cooking depletes and even destroys certain nutrients in foods, because they are vulnerable to the heat, air, and water that are an important part of cooking.

You couldn't play it safer. So long as the food is fresh and from unpolluted sources, eating "in the raw" is a remarkably healthy way of eating. All the nutrition is intact. Proteins are in first-class condition. Vitamins vulnerable to heat, water, and air are preserved. Minerals too are at their best. Enzymes, the nutritional catalysts, are sparkling and alive in raw foods, but totally destroyed in cooking.

As our knowledge of nutrition evolves, one thing is absolutely clear: Natural foods in their freshest, most natural state contain a natural balance of nutrients that make them work their best for your body. Raw fresh foods may be even more vital than we now realize. Nutrition is, after all, a young science; vitamins were isolated a mere fifty years ago!

Would you like to know more about exactly which nutrients are affected in specific foods you enjoy? The U.S. Department of Agriculture has all the answers in a handbook called *Composition of Foods, Raw, Cooked and Processed.* This is the definitive, authoritative source of food and nutrition information, used by all the top food professionals and home economists. All you do is send $3.60 to the address below and you'll have the answers to most of your nutrition questions handy, right in your kitchen, whenever you need to look something up. Write to U.S. Department of Agriculture, Handbook #8, Supt. of Documents, Government Printing Office, Washington, D.C. 20402.

Raw foods are quick and easy to prepare. Take away that stove and oven time, and you have gourmet eating a lot faster. Raw-food dishes are prepared with very fresh foods, at the height of their flavor, so a minimum of fussing and flavor-adding is needed. Most raw-food recipes are designed to showcase the foods themselves, since nature does most of the work for you.

In this era of convenience foods, we should not forget that the original and very best convenience foods are those produced by nature. Look at it this way: If you save 20 minutes a day (a conservative estimate) by serving one or two raw food dishes, that adds up to 6 days a year. That's a mini-vacation. If you save an hour a day, that's 15 free days a year! And you're not cutting down on quality—you're expanding your food horizons. *The more we fuss over food, the better it is* is an old wives' tale. It's just not so.

Raw foods save energy—yours and your country's. The days of cheap energy, whether gas, electricity, water, or human labor, are gone forever. We live in a changing society, in which we all must learn to share and conserve our energy. Raw-food eating is an inspired way to cope with any energy crises you can think of.

Think of it: no cooking, no pot-scrubbing, no fuss and bother. All those steadily increasing utility bills for gas, electricity, and water that we pay every month are chargeable to cooking 3 times a day, 365 days a year, in many homes. That's an amazing 1,095 energy-consuming sessions in your kitchen a year! If you skip cooking and eat more raw-food dishes, you can save a whopping amount of money on utility bills.

Raw foods are excellent for your digestion. Logically, and not surprisingly, raw foods are outstanding for maintaining and often restoring good digestion. Unless you have a health problem that requires a special diet, raw-food cuisine is ideal for you, with all the natural nutrients delicately balanced the way nature meant them to be and all the natural fibers, widely publicized recently, that help to digest foods efficiently. Fruits and vegetables are particularly high in natural fiber. And if you eat a moderate amount of raw foods, perhaps one or more at each meal, you may never need another laxative. All raw fruits, dried fruits (prunes, etc.), raw vegetables, nuts, yogurt, and cultured dairy products are excellent in this respect.

Raw foods are a great way to stay slim. The more raw food you eat, the less likely you are to gain weight. It's got more bulk, takes more time to chew and eat, calls for fewer fattening sauces and ingredients. It is also more filling, and automatically steers you clear of eating junk food or empty calories. Not a single calorie is wasted.

Raw food has other subtle ways of helping you lead a slim life. Since it is always nutritious, it tends to satisfy those hunger pangs that force you to overeat. It is indeed a bountiful new world for dieters; you soon discover that the fruits and berries taste even better with a tiny bit of sugar than they do in a calorie-laden slice of pie. And rich sauces and gravies are hardly missed when the foods themselves are full of juicy flavor.

All raw foods are "beauty" foods. Because they are so nutritious, and so healthful for digestion, raw foods promote healthy, glowing skin and sparkling eyes.

Raw foods are good for your teeth. Tooth decay from refined sugar and overprocessed foods just doesn't happen with raw food. Raw foods have all their natural chewiness intact, with fibers and textures that literally brush your teeth and massage your gums while you're enjoying their good flavors.

Even more appealing are all the luscious natural sugars that occur in many raw foods, especially fruits and vegetables. These natural sugars satisfy your cravings for sugar without causing tooth decay. As the American Dental Association will be happy to assure you (why not write for one of their recommended food lists?), the fresher the food, the better. Many of the recipes in the dessert section of this book call for small amounts of sugar because our palates are accustomed to sugared desserts. But when fruits are naturally sweet, try skipping the sugar completely. You often don't need it.

Raw foods are wonderful for children. Not because they're healthy, but because they taste good! Most of those children who make faces at cooked vegetables will happily gobble them raw. Their young systems have built-in nutrition signals that tell them raw vegetables are good to eat. Often it's because fresh, tender young raw fruits and vegetables taste of natural sugar, that good flavor children instinctively love. And, of course, from birth on children love the nutritious goodness of all fresh dairy foods. Perhaps most important, eating raw foods instead of sugared cereals and cakes sets the pattern for lifelong habits of good nutrition.

Raw food is a creative experience. Go ahead and experiment with raw food, with the greatest of ease. Surely one of the most powerful of raw food's advantages is how much men enjoy the gourmet world of raw foods, and how happily children take to it. It is convenient for everyone in a family. Experiments are usually good, and often positively inspired. And you'll find raw foods so colorful and easy to work with that beautiful presentations and eye-catching garnishing touches come naturally. Try new sauces and dips; try combining raw foods the way you combine favorite cooked foods. If you have a delicious fresh food to start with, it's hard to go wrong.

Raw food is for singles or a crowd. Raw food is deliciously convenient, no matter how many you're "not cooking" for. For one or two people, raw food lends itself handsomely to both gourmet and simple meals. (Some raw food suppers take literally seconds to prepare!) For entertaining, or large families, raw food is even more at home. Sumptuous displays are dramatic and colorful with raw foods, and often the time in the kitchen is cut to a welcome minimum.

All of these raw-food advantages are good to know about, but surely the most important delight about the world of raw foods is the taste. Raw foods are simply delicious.

In addition to their health advantages and superb taste, raw foods are also easy to select and work with. There are just a few general rules that you should keep in mind:

SHOPPING FOR RAW FOODS
How you shop for raw foods is very important. The great chefs of the world freely admit that part of their art is selecting only the choicest

of ingredients: the finest quality, the meatiest, the sun-ripened, the vine-ripened, the youngest, the plumpest, and so on. All of these nuances influence the flavor of fresh raw foods. If fine ingredients are the hallmark of great cooking, so they are the essence of gourmet raw-food eating.

These are skills you learn to do by doing. Many shopping suggestions for specific foods are given in this book, but here are a few basic rules. Use the best produce markets, fresh-fish sources, dedicated butchers. Seek out the most luxurious, expensive stores *first,* not so much to buy (especially if price is an object with you) as to learn. Just wandering around looking at the very best raw foods is an education in itself. If you can, buy just a few of the ones you want to taste. You can then pop into your local supermarket and cannily move in on their most superb offerings.

Remember, a cosmetic look or perfect symmetry is not always a sign of goodness. Nature is not an assembly line. Many fine fruits and vegetables are uneven in size and have little marks on them, especially those organically grown.

Favor younger-looking, brighter-colored vegetables. Baby-sized vegetables are often super for eating raw. When in doubt, *taste.* Buy just one of three or four foods, then taste them all and buy lots more of the best. Taste-testing is particularly good with fruits, which tend to vary in size and flavor from season to season. If a fruit is fragrant, that's a good sign. If it's mushy, that's disaster.

Ask the produce man. Ask the fish man, and the butcher. They are always-informative and sometimes-inspired sources of raw-food know-how. And, like all professionals, they love to be consulted. A clever produce man showed me how to make a pineapple boat one day, much to my delight. After years of hacking away ineptly at pineapples, I was suddenly a skilled performer.

KITCHEN EQUIPMENT

About the only thing you *have* to have is a *very* sharp knife and a sharpening stone from the hardware store. If you don't know how to use the stone, ask the man in the hardware store to show you. Once demonstrated, it's easy.

Ideally, you should also have several more small sharp knives, a coring knife, a large chopping knife for mincing, a slit-middle paring knife, and a curved grapefruit knife for cantaloupe, grapefruit, pineapple, and the like.

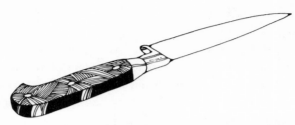

If you're interested, there are clever cutting and sculpturing tools such as melon ballers available. The new food processors perform all sorts of cutting and shredding tasks beautifully. They are a joy, but not a necessity if your family is small. A blender and an electric mixer are also big helps.

CLEANING RAW FOODS

Raw foods must be clean as well as fresh. You don't have to carry this to extremes, but most raw foods should be washed thoroughly and soaked for no more than 1 or 2 minutes in cold water. Use a little wire brush or a plastic Tuffy pad to help with cleaning, if needed. Foods should be patted or shaken free of excess moisture and kept in a cool place, away from light, or in a refrigerator. Many raw foods come obligingly sealed in their own disposable shells and need little cleaning.

SEASONING RAW FOODS

The less seasoning, the better. Since raw fresh foods vary appreciably in flavor from season to season and from region to region, taste as you go along. Seasonings such as salt and sugar exist naturally in many raw foods.

RAW FOODS TO EAT IN MODERATION

The composition of a few raw foods is such that they should be eaten in moderation. Spinach, Swiss chard, and beet greens, before cooking, contain oxalic acid, which, eaten in large amounts, often can briefly inhibit the body's ability to absorb calcium and magnesium. Enjoy those fabulous spinach salads, but not every day. Hearty root vegetables, such as beets, carrots, and turnips, are great tossed into green salads, but the combined fiber in a large "roots" salad can produce laxative-type results. Raw egg whites contain a substance that can interfere briefly with absorption of some nutrients, so limit yourself to one raw egg a day, or two every other day.

FOODS THAT SHOULD NEVER BE EATEN RAW

Virtually all foods are meant to be eaten raw—but "virtually" is not the same as "all." Besides the obvious (such as unfamiliar wild mushrooms), avoid:

- any food that is no longer quite fresh
- any food from a contaminated source
- freshwater fish and poultry (not recommended in the United States)
- pork and pork products (except fine raw-cured hams from sources of known quality)
- meats that have been in contact with pork-contaminated surfaces, such as grinders used for pork (have your steak-tartare meat ground to order by a reputable butcher while you watch, or grind your own at home)
- shellfish (shrimp, crab, lobster, crayfish, etc.) are rarely recommended in the U.S.
- any saltwater fish from polluted shore waters (check with your local fishing commission)
- rhubarb (contains excessive oxalic acid)
- unfamiliar wild leaves and roots and berries (many are great, some are poisonous, so don't experiment)
- foods purchased from farms where human "night soil" is used. (more likely in foreign countries, but conceivable here)
- prepackaged supermarket meat and fish (these are good for cooking, but for raw eating have meats cut to order and purchase fish from a source that specializes in quality *fresh* fish)

As you can see from the above, the don'ts in raw-food eating are very few.

THE SENSUAL WORLD OF RAW FOODS

Raw food has always been fashionable. The most elegant restaurants all over the world long ago discovered that the most perfect of their local foods were superbly delicious in their raw, natural state, thinly sliced, artfully presented, sublimely sauced, and often outrageously priced.

Today, with the new methods of year-round growing and sophisticated shipping techniques, raw-food cuisine need no longer be the province of elegant restaurants but can move into the kitchen. Delicious, nutritious, an elegant way to eat and to entertain, raw foods are also truly sensual in their looks and tastes. Think of Roman emperors toying with grapes, of lovers escaping to dappled forests with a picnic basket of fresh fruits and cheeses. And what could be more glamorous than sliced fruits in champagne?

Raw food is even sexy. It's true! Most of the most famous "sex foods" are raw: oysters, olives, cavier, nuts, avocados, tender fruits. These foods are sensual, in that they appeal to all of our senses—and sexy, in that they are potently nutritious.

And there is a subtle sensuality in all raw-food cuisine that we find very appealing. Raw food truly satiates. It is a beautiful way to eat, but also satisfies our appetites. Our senses and our stomachs are pleased. Eating becomes an esthetic act.

For all these reasons, raw foods are indeed a fascinating and delicious world. Hopefully, the recipes in this book will help you revel in their delectable flavors.

2. SPECTACULARS

EACH OF THESE RECIPES has a special flair to it that makes it especially interesting. Together they give you a taste and a preview of the boundless panorama of delicious raw-food eating in this book: old-fashioned dishes, gourmet classics, internationally famous dishes, and some simple, no-preparation offerings that are dramatic, striking, and colorful. All are showpieces meant for entertaining.

BAGNA CAUDA

This is a summer extravaganza in Italy. Literally translated, "bagna cauda" means "hot bath." In a most unusual presentation, raw vegetables are partially cut through, heaped in a big wooden salad bowl or on a big wooden tray, and served with a hot bath of a dip that sizzles with salty, spicy, buttery excitement. Each person breaks away slices, spears them with a fork, and immerses them, fondue style, in the hot dip. Truly, this is the Godfather of dips, but with a savory rather than unsavory past. It is a creation of the Piedmont area of Italy.

VEGETABLES

½ small cabbage, red or white,
   sliced partway through
1 medium cauliflower, cored
1 carrot per person, cut partway
   through in slices
young string beans, tips removed
whole cherry tomatoes, stems on
1 green pepper, cored, with
   vertical slits partway
   through
6 mushrooms, stems trimmed but
   not removed, with vertical
   slits partway through (or
   12–18 whole small
   mushrooms)

10 radishes
2 turnips, small, scrubbed and
   sliced partway through
2 yellow crookneck squash, sliced
   partway through
2 zucchini, sliced partway through
1 bunch green onions (scallions),
   trimmed, with part of the
   green left on

DIP

1 can flat anchovy fillets, drained
¼ cup olive oil
¼ pound butter
5 small cloves garlic, pressed or
   crushed

2 shallots, minced (optional)
salt (very optional, since anchovies are so salty)

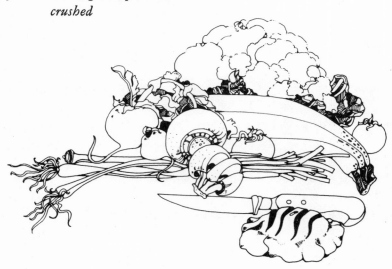

Prepare washed and trimmed vegetables as indicated, cutting deeply enough so slices can be broken away by hand (but not so deep that vegetables fall in slices). Arrange vegetables in a salad bowl or on a platter.

Mash anchovies with a little oil until smooth. Then add remaining dip ingredients, heat, and stir. Do not boil; the mixture must not get hot enough to burn on the bottom.

Serve at once, in the cooking pot, a chafing dish, or an electric warmer set for fondue. Napkins must be provided, along with forks or spears for dipping. The dip container must be shallow enough so people can stir down to the rich flavor at the bottom (the anchovy mixture tends to sink). The buttery, salty warmth of the hot bath plays against the cool crispness of the vegetables with mouth-watering results.

SERVES 6–10

Some will eat 2 cups of vegetables, some less. The dip makes it temptingly easy to eat a lot, and the low calorie content of most raw vegetables tends to remove inhibitions.

CAVIAR

Which came first, the chicken or the egg?

When it comes to caviar, perhaps this should be changed to: Which came first, the fish or the egg? The point is that caviar, the eggs of fish, is a legendary source food prized throughout the world. It is traditionally eaten raw, only lightly salted or marinated. The many caviars sold in the United States are preserved in such a way as to retain the delicate, impossibly tender and appealing flavor.

The eggs of the sea come from many fish. Some caviar is black and gleaming, some is gray, some has been darkened for visual appeal, and some, such as salmon caviar, is rosy red. Each provides a special pleasure. The most famous of all caviar comes from the huge, noble sturgeon that swim the rivers of Russia. Mollosol caviar is often flown, very fresh, delicately and precisely iced, directly from Russia to eager recipients, both private and restaurant, all over the world. If you can be blasé about two hundred dollars a pound, this is the caviar for you.

For those of us who cannot afford or do not choose to spend two hundred dollars a pound, there is a variety of sumptuous alternatives, for caviar is, after all, found in many fish. Lumpfish caviar is very popular, and so fresh and delicious that it's impossible to think of a better dish.

One of caviar's greatest virtues is that it is quite effortless to serve. No cooking is dreamed of, and fussing with minced hard-cooked egg and chopped onion is actually sneered at by the true caviar purist (although secretly enjoyed by many of us.)

Caviar is, of course, quite nourishing.

And what other food costing sixteen dollars a pound can you consume with a comfortable feeling of thrift?

CLASSIC CAVIAR

2 ounces caviar, chilled
20–30 mild-flavored wafers or crackers (the caviar seller can suggest complementary crackers)

Set the caviar, in a chilled dish, in a basin of crushed or shaved ice. Serve with the wafers or crackers and a knife. Optional accompaniments include side bowls of unsalted butter, minced hard-cooked egg, and minced onion.

SERVES 2–4

CAVIAR CANAPÉS

½ cup unsalted butter
round wafers or crackers
2 ounces black caviar

Allow butter to soften. Shortly before serving, spread the outer edges of each cracker with a ring of butter ⅛″–¼″ wide. Spread center with caviar. Chill 15 minutes.

SERVES 2–4

CAVIAR PIE

You can make this in the morning and bring it out, with its elegant topping of shimmering black caviar, when you're ready for pre-dinner revelry.

4–6 hard-cooked eggs, chopped	*mayonnaise*
½–1 onion, finely chopped	*8 ounces cream cheese*
⅛ teaspoon salt (or to taste)	*4 ounces (2 little jars) black*
pepper	*lumpfish caviar*

Mix together chopped eggs, onion, salt, pepper, and enough mayonnaise to hold it together nicely. Press this mixture into the bottom of a pie plate, smoothing out to make even. Put it in the freezer for 10–15 minutes, or until it is fairly firm. Meanwhile, whip cream cheese until smooth and soft (leaving it out for an hour before you whip makes it easier). Spread cream cheese on top of the egg mixture. If cheese layer is extremely soft, put it in the refrigerator for a few minutes; then make an even top layer of caviar. Refrigerate till serving time.

To serve as an appetizer, cut the pie and let all help themselves. Serve with dark pumpernickel bread or crackers. For a first course, serve individual slices on small plates and pass crackers or bread.

SERVES 4–6

WHEEL OF CHEESE, WREATH OF GRAPES

For parties, the ultimate in nonextravagant excitement is a whole wheel of cheese. After years of gazing, stupefied with admiration, at those beautiful wheels in cheese shops, I finally realized I was spending as much money to buy a lot of small amounts of cheese, which I had to fuss over, as I would if I bought one huge wheel.

A pleasant after-the-party thought: Any remaining cheese can be refrigerated or frozen for later.

Consider:

• A wheel of Brie floating like a full moon on a dark wooden platter,

served with pale crackers and sliced apples.
- A wheel of grape cheese topped with pale green grapes, served with toast points kept warm.
- A wheel of Roquefort crowned with deep purple grapes, served with pristine rows of very plain stone-ground wheat crackers and small loaves of French bread.

Set out the cheese, looking opulent beyond belief, with an array of different, interesting crackers and breads. Top the wheel with a beautiful bunch of whatever grapes are in season.

A POUND OF CHEESE SERVES 5–8 PEOPLE

FIRE AND ICE

Candles flicker invitingly amid a bed of shimmering, crisp raw vegetables and olives—lovely to look at, and the vegetables stay nice and chilly.

> *1 bunch radishes*
> *1 can pitted black olives*
> *1 cauliflower, broken into flowerets*
> *1 box cherry tomatoes*

Clean and chill vegetables. Just before serving, fill a large chilled bowl (a salad bowl will do) with crushed ice to within 1″ of top. Insert 6–10 very thin dripless candles (up to ½″ at base, 9″–12″ long) into the ice in a scattered pattern; press ice around bases until firm. Cluster a layer of vegetables and olives around candles on ice. Light candles and serve. This will burn glamorously for at least 2 hours at a party. Refill with more vegetables whenever necessary. Put a bowl of dip alongside (see Index), or simply seasoned salt.

SERVES 6–10

SALADE CHAMPIGNONS
MUSHROOM SALAD

I went mad with delight when I first ate this salad at Au Petit Café, a marvelous French restaurant—and with frustration when I tried, with no success, to duplicate it at home, using cooked mushrooms. Later I found out that the secret is *very* fresh raw mushrooms. When you shop, look to see that the pale mushroom gills on the underside are closed. When the dark brown underside of the cap is revealed, the mushroom is too old for gourmet raw dishes.

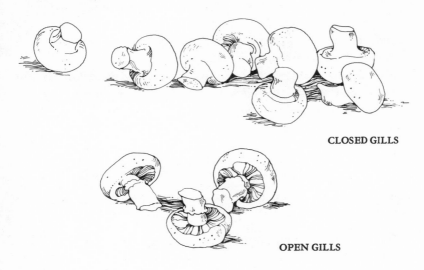

CLOSED GILLS

OPEN GILLS

Despite its simplicity, this is a rich salad, sumptuous enough for the very best dinner parties.

1 head Boston lettuce, chilled and torn into bite-size pieces
20–25 medium mushrooms, sliced
2 tablespoons finely minced parsley
½ cup vinaigrette dressing (see Index), made with wine vinegar and
*   olive oil mixed with a milder oil*

Arrange lettuce on chilled plates. In separate bowls, toss mushrooms and parsley in dressing; taste for seasoning and heap on lettuce. Drizzle with any remaining dressing. Serve as salad side dish, or as a separate course with very dry champagne or white wine.

SERVES 4

SMORGASBORD

This ancient Scandinavian way of serving fresh foods was one of the earliest of buffets, and the Scandinavians perfected the decorative art of the buffet generations ago. Smorgasbord was once popular in America, but World War II food shortages caused a decline in the extravagant smorgasbord tradition. Now it has returned, in a less opulent but still exquisite form. Single smorgasbord-style dishes are often served for their beauty as well as their taste.

Here is a sampling, two smorgasbord classics that go beautifully with raw-vegetable displays and demonstrate the orderly beauty of decorative Scandinavian cold cuisine.

THE ANCHOVY EYE

This appetizer originated in Sweden. It is colorful and easy to prepare.

> *1 egg yolk*
> *1–2 tablespoons minced onion*
> *8 anchovy fillets, minced*

Chill a handsome small serving plate. Place the egg yolk in the center; arrange minced onion in a ring around the yolk and anchovies in a ring next to the onion. Set out crackers or toast points kept warm in oven till serving time. The first person to help himself stirs all ingredients together, blending well.

This dish also looks attractive served on a wooden board and garnished with a wedge of lemon.

SERVES 4

FAGELBO
BIRD'S NEST

5 anchovy fillets, chopped   *2 tablespoons diced pickled beets*
1 tablespoon chopped onion   *1 tablespoon diced cold boiled potato*
1 tablespoon capers   *2 egg yolks*
1 tablespoon chopped chives

Put the first six ingredients in separate mounds on a small serving plate, arranging them so that they form one or two small nestlike circles. Depress the center of the mounds slightly and carefully place an egg yolk in each depression, to give you a filled "bird's nest." Chill. If dish is prepared ahead of time, cover with aluminum foil and refrigerate until serving time.

The first person to help himself at serving time (perhaps it could be you) stirs all the ingredients together until mixed. For a buffet, a small helping is spooned out onto each person's dinner plate. For an appetizer, pass tiny, thin-sliced Swedish or Danish rye bread.

SERVES 4

KATHRYN'S ARTISTIC
TABOULI

Tabouli is a distinctive Eastern salad made from fine bulghur (cracked wheat) soaked in chicken stock or water, then marinated in a luscious array of chopped greens, tomato, and a dressing that can be as lemony as you can take it. Increase the lemon juice with a light touch if you are unaccustomed to the Eastern passion for lemon.

*2 cups bulghur, soaked for 2 hours
    in chicken stock or water
    and squeezed very dry in
    cloth
1½–2 cups chopped green onion
1½–2 cups finely chopped parsley
¾ cup peeled, chopped tomatoes
salt and pepper to taste
1 cup olive oil*

*⅓ (or more) cup lemon juice, to
    taste
1 teaspoon chopped mint or sweet
    basil (optional)
black olives, tomato wedges,
    lemon wedges, lemon-
    peel rings, and/or parsley
    sprigs for garnish*

Mix all but the garnish gently in a salad bowl until dressing is absorbed. Smooth the surface and mound in the center, then garnish. Marinate in refrigerator for one-half to 3 hours. Plant a cluster of parsley in the center when served.

At a buffet, tabouli can be spooned onto plates along with other buffet foods. With cocktails, it can be dipped up on small inner romaine leaves, pita bread, or crackers.

SERVES 10

TAHINI SESAME DIP WITH PITA

Although oil wells receive more publicity, culinary treats from the Middle East are fast becoming favorite American foods. Pita, the wonderful pancake-looking bread now found in many big-city markets, and its accompanying tahini dip may never replace the taco, but they're certainly trying. If pita is not available, try pumpernickel, French bread, or interesting crackers.

Tahini is actually a sesame "cream"—water and sesame seeds blended together. The paste is a bit like mayonnaise with a wonderful sesame flavor.

*1 cup sesame seeds
1½ cups water
2 cloves garlic, crushed
dash cayenne pepper
1 teaspoon salt
juice of 1–2 lemons (or limes), to taste*

*3 tablespoons olive oil
2 tablespoons chopped
    parsley
1 7-oz. can black olives
pita bread*

Combine sesame seeds and 1 cup water in a blender and whirl until fluffy. Mix with garlic, ½ cup water, cayenne pepper, salt, and lemon juice. Mixture should be creamy; add a little water if it is too thick. Serve on small plates with a swirl of olive oil, a sprinkling of parsley, and several olives, accompanied by pita.

SERVES 2–4

Besides the fun of pita dipping and the good flavor, tahini has other advantages. From a nutrition standpoint, sesame seeds—the base of tahini—rank with milk as a top source of protein, calcium, and phosphorus.

PROSCIUTTO, MELON, AND FIG PLATTER

Just the thing for summer wine parties.

⅔ pound prosciutto, sliced paper-thin
1 cantaloupe, cut in bars about 2" by
¾" by ½"
½ honeydew melon, cut the
same way

½ Persian (or other) melon,
cut the same way
4 figs, quartered

Wrap a piece of prosciutto around each piece of melon and fig, then spear with a toothpick to hold it together. Chill. At serving time, line a big platter or a small table with big green ivy or tree leaves and display the assorted prosciutto-wrapped fruits. Come winter, you can substitute pears for the figs and use winter melons.

SERVES 8–12

CHLODNIK

This is a smashing conversation piece, a pink panther of a soup based on the classic beet-and-yogurt chlodnik. Serve it simply or with bowls of chopped goodies for elaborate occasions. This is a cool but hearty dish, good summer and winter.

1 cup cucumber, peeled and seeded
1 teaspoon finely minced parsley
1 teaspoon finely minced chives (or
green onion tops)
½ cup cooked beets, peeled
1 clove garlic

1 cup yogurt
2 cups milk (or part milk, part
cream or sour cream)
salt, if needed
croutons, diced cucumber, diced
beets (all optional)

Set cucumber, parsley, and chives aside. Whirl next five ingredients in blender until smooth. Add cucumber and blend for 5 seconds, until cucumber is chopped but not puréed. Stir in parsley and chives. Taste for seasoning, adding more milk or salt or cucumber as you wish. Chill for at least an hour. Serve in chilled soup bowls, with pretty cucumber slices floating on the creamy pink surface of the soup. Pass bowls of croutons, diced cucumber, beets, etc., for spooning on top.

SERVES 6–8

FILET MIGNON TARTARE SCANDINAVIAN

This recipe is inspired by Scandia, surely one of the world's best restaurants. One taste and you understand why they've been raving about steak tartare all these centuries. While steak tartare is every bit as delicious made with sirloin and top round, for special occasions only the pampered elegance of filet mignon will do. To make this dish, the filet mignon is scraped, not ground. The effect is a tender texture all its own that absorbs the accompaniments with subtle perfection.

1½ pounds lean filet mignon,
freshly cut
parsley for garnish
2 tablespoons grated fresh horse-
radish
2 egg yolks
3 tablespoons olive oil
1 teaspoon wine vinegar

1 tablespoon minced onion
salt and pepper, to taste
¾ tablespoon Worcestershire
sauce
2 tablespoons capers
2 tablespoons slivered pickled
beets (optional)
1 teaspoon Grey Poupon mustard

Shop for your filet mignon carefully. Detailed instructions are given on page 65. Place filet on a cutting board. Chill 6 plates, and garnish each plate with parsley and a teaspoon of grated horseradish. Bring them to table with the rest of the ingredients. Put egg yolks in a bowl.

Scraping the filet: With a sharp medium-size knife, scrape with the grain of the meat, at an angle so that knife edge pushes, or scrapes, the meat away from the grain. It takes a few minutes, so work patiently.

At the table: Whip the egg yolks vigorously with a wire whisk. Still whisking, add the olive oil, drop by drop, then the wine vinegar, mustard, minced onion, salt and pepper, and Worcestershire sauce. Now add filet to sauce in bowl and toss very gently with two forks. Sprinkle with capers and beets and toss again until barely mixed. Place a serving on each of the chilled plates and garnish with additional parsley and horseradish. Make a crisscross pattern with the tines of the fork on each serving.

Serve this with a good red wine, crusty rolls, and a flourish.

SERVES 6

SEVICHE
SEAFOOD BUFFET

Seviche (sometimes spelled Ceviche), the South American raw-fish dish marinated to tender perfection in lime juice, combines fish fillets with shrimp, scallops, and rows of tiny fresh clams to create a really dazzling cold buffet, or the entree at a dinner party or outdoor uncookout.

Everything is cold, and waits obligingly in the refrigerator. A few minutes before serving, you simply arrange the various seafoods on a big, chilled platter and serve with assorted breads, perhaps a cold rice or hot corn dish, and a very simple romaine salad.

SEAFOOD

1½ pounds sea-bass fillets (or halibut, red snapper, or other white-fish
    fillets)
¾ pound scallops, raw
24 small clams on the half shell
12–24 medium shrimp, fresh or frozen, boiled and shelled

MARINADE

juice of 4–6 limes
1½ teaspoons sugar
3 teaspoons salt
1½ teaspoons pepper
6 dashes hot pepper sauce
    (Tabasco, etc.)
½ teaspoon oregano

¼ cup olive oil
1 green pepper, minced
3 tomatoes, peeled and chopped
1 cucumber, cut into half slices,
    and ½ bunch parsley
    sprigs for garnish

Purchase seafood from a fine market that specializes in very fresh fish, and tell them you are going to make a marinated-raw dish. Cut fish fillets into bite-size pieces (½″) and immerse fish pieces and scallops in lime juice, turning gently. There should be enough lime juice to almost cover the top layer. Cover and marinate in refrigerator for 3 hours. Add rest of marinade ingredients to seviches mixture and return to refrigerator. Scrub the clams under cold running water (do not soak) with a stiff wire brush, cleaning carefully where shell closes. Refrigerate in bowl. Devein boiled, shelled shrimp and refrigerate.

Three hours before serving, tumble shrimp gently into seviches fish mixture, and let them marinate until serving time. Open clams by inserting a small sharp knife near the hinge or mid-back of clam, and then moving knife edge into lip of clam. Twist and leverage will open clamshell. Put a large platter in the freezer to become icy-cold.

Just before serving, arrange fish fillets, scallops, shrimp, and opened clams in separate rows on the platter. Fill in with cucumber slices between the rows. If you have extra space on the platter, fill it with quartered tomatoes or hard-cooked eggs, or parsley.

This is a pale, shimmering, yet colorful platter, with its bits of red tomato and green pepper, pale-pink shrimp, and snowy-white fish.

The kinds of fish and their proportions in this recipe can be varied to suit the season and the fish available in your region. (For more on seviches, the marinade way with raw fish traditional all over South America, see Index.)

SERVES 6–8

SALMON TARTARE WITH CAVIAR

This is truly rapturously delicious. The salmon must be a superbly fresh fillet or steak. It makes a lovely main course, preceded perhaps by a creamy chlodnik soup (see Index) and followed by a watercress salad (see Index) and dessert. Ideally, it should be served with aquavit on ice. For this at-home version, we have Michel of Scandia Restaurant to thank.

1 ⅓ pounds salmon fillets
butter
2 large slices pumpernickel bread
2 egg yolks
2 ounces black caviar
1 tablespoon olive oil
juice of 1 lemon
1 scant tablespoon Worcestershire
  sauce

1 ½ tablespoons capers
1 tablespoon minced onion
1 ½ teaspoons Grey Poupon
  mustard
a dash of salt if desired
ground pepper

Mince the salmon very fine. Butter pumpernickel smoothly to the edges, then top with salmon. Press 2 hollows into top of salmon, and into each put an egg yolk. Sprinkle caviar lavishly on top of egg yolks and salmon. Bring the plate of caviar-topped salmon to the table, along with a well-chilled bowl, the rest of the ingredients, and a wire whisk.

At the table, spoon egg yolks gently from salmon into icy bowl, then whip vigorously with the whisk. Add the olive oil, drop by drop, beating hard until it forms a thin mayonnaiselike sauce. Gently whisk in lemon juice, Worcestershire sauce, capers, onion, mustard, salt, and pepper. Now remove the salmon from the buttered bread and toss gently in the sauce with two forks until just mixed. Taste for seasoning (a joyous moment). Cut pumpernickel into 4 pieces. Place salmon tartare evenly on each piece. Make a casual crisscross pattern on top with the tines of a fork. Garnish with a bit of lettuce, pour the aquavit, and skoal!

SERVES 4

Note: If you prefer a less dramatic presentation mix Salmon Tartare in kitchen and serve on bread.

COBB SALAD IN THE BROWN DERBY MANNER

Originally popularized by Irvin Cobb in the '30s and '40s at the Hollywood Brown Derby, Cobb Salad has been nibbled on by probably every movie star that you can think of. It comes to the table minced to an astonishingly fine degree, in a colorful array to be tossed with dressing while you watch. Here is one of the many reverent imitations. (Authentically, this salad is minced very, very fine, but it is also good chopped, or cut into thin strips, chiffonade style.)

½ *head lettuce*	*1 avocado*
1 small bunch chicory	*3 hard-cooked eggs*
1 small bunch watercress	*2 tablespoons chopped chives or*
⅓ *head romaine*	*green onions*
2 medium tomatoes, peeled	⅓ *cup grated Romano cheese*
2 breasts of chicken, poached in	*1 cup vinaigrette dressing (see*
broth and chilled	*Index) with pinch of*
6 strips crisp bacon	*sugar*

Chop everything up very finely. Heap greens in bottom of salad bowl and arrange other ingredients in waves on top. Pour on dressing and toss at the table so all can enjoy the pretty colors. And then savor the sumptuous flavor.

SERVES 6

TOSSED SALAD ANTIPASTO

Traditional Italian antipasto is a before-dinner affair, an irresistible array of cold meats, fishes, marinated dishes, and iced raw vegetables.

But here the appealing flavors of antipasto become the dinner itself, in a salad as stunning to look at as it is to eat. Bold Italian greens topped with tuna, anchovies, and salami make this a hearty, mouthwatering main dish. Serve it with big hunks of Italian bread, unsalted butter, and cups of minestrone soup, followed by an Italian dessert like biscuit tortoni (see Index).

6–8 large handfuls of romaine, chicory, and escarole (1 handful per person)
2 7-oz. cans white tuna packed in water
1 2½-oz. can anchovy fillets
6–8 slices salami, cut into slivers
2 hard-cooked eggs, sliced
1 tomato, cut into eighths

½ large red onion, sliced into half rings (or leek rings or white onions)
½ can pitted black olives
¼ cup finely chopped parsley
1 jar marinated artichoke hearts (optional)
10 large radishes, sliced
1 cup oil-and-vinegar dressing (see Index)

Wash, dry, and chill greens. Tear romaine into big pieces; shred chicory and escarole into smaller pieces (they are a bit stronger-flavored). Heap greens in bottom of salad bowl. Mound tuna in center and surround with other ingredients, each fanning out like a pie slice. Cover and chill until serving. Bring salad to the table to be admired, then pour on dressing and toss at table. Taste for seasoning.

SERVES 6–8

CUCUMBER-TOMATO-ONION BUFFET

Four people can do away with a giant plate of this spread for a casual feast. As a buffet platter with other foods, it is striking. This is a way of serving familiar, everyday, favorite foods and making them look exciting and sumptuous.

5 tomatoes, peeled and chopped
1 cup finely chopped green onions
(1 1/4 bunches)
3 large cucumbers, peeled and diced

1 1/2 cups mayonnaise (see Index)
1 loaf French bread, sliced

Peeling the tomatoes is easier if you dip them in boiling water for a scant minute. Refrigerate cut-up tomatoes, onions, and cucumbers in separate bowls. Just before serving, heap mayonnaise in the center of a large platter, with a ring of onions all around it; then make another ring of cucumbers, and a final ring of tomatoes. Around the outside rim of platter, arrange the slices of French bread. Serve with small plates, napkins, and some salt and pepper.

SERVES 4

PALE WINE, PALE CHEESE, PALE FRUITS
A COUNTRY FEAST

Collect an assortment of the following and assemble for an instant, casual, but very sumptuous Sunday brunch, summer dinner, or luncheon. It's also an easy dish for office lunches at the conference table when you want something simple but very dramatic. The feeling is that of a French picnic, Provence style.

a good dry white wine
green grapes (in season)
pale-green pears
pale Golden Delicious apples
deep-green Kelsey pears
yellow pears
a grapefruit
pale creamy cheeses: Brie, Port Salut, Swiss, green-streaked Roquefort, and blue—anything that echoes the colors of white wine and green grapes
cream cheese

stalks of very-pale-green celery, stacked in a glass with crushed ice in bottom
a few stalks of Belgian endive, with vinaigrette sauce on the side
pale avocado slices in vinaigrette sauce
a pale, creamy-colored bread— perhaps a soy bread, or pale French rolls
pale, unsalted butter crushed into a pot

Allow about 2 fruits, 4 slices of bread, ¼ pound cheese, ⅛ pound cream cheese, and several slices or stalks of vegetables per person.

SERVES 6

Note: Since nothing is cooked, leftovers are really not leftovers, but good food for another meal. If you use paper plates, cleaning up is simple, too.

BRILLIANT FALL/WINTER COUNTRY FEAST

If it's fall or winter, you might try assembling a similar feast based on the color of red wine, with dark breads, red apples, cranberry spreads, grape cheeses and orangy cheeses, radishes and tomatoes, and so on. Sliced salami or other meats might also be added.

SWEET CREAM CHEESE AND FRUIT WHIP

Berries, cherries, and sliced fruits surround this billowing whip on a big plate. It's absolutely gorgeous and quite easy to prepare. Guests love it, because they can gorge themselves on just the fruits they want.

FRUITS

1½ cups Bing cherries	4 figs, apricots, or what-have-you,
1½ cups berries or grapes	quartered
5 small plums, halved, with pits	3 apples, peeled, cored, and sliced
removed	3 pears, cored and sliced
	(optional)

DIP

8 ounces cream cheese, softened	½ cup heavy cream, whipped
½ cup milk	bittersweet chocolate, grated
2 tablespoons sugar	(optional)
splash vanilla	

Refrigerate fruits after brushing cut surfaces with lemon juice. Prepare dip by mixing cream cheese with milk, sugar, and vanilla; then blend whipped cream in gently. Serve dip in bowl, with chocolate grated on top, surrounded by fruits in pretty groups on huge platter.

SERVES 6–10

Variation: For an extravagant one-fruit piece, buy 1 *perfect* fruit in appropriate quantity and follow same directions.

FRUIT AND CHEESE FONDUE

This is nice for casual get-togethers, tennis Sundays, or evening affairs. Surround the fondue pot with this panorama of fruits. Each chunk of fruit is speared, then dipped into the hot melted-cheese fondue.

FONDUE

> *1½ pounds cheddar cheese, grated*
> *¼–½ cup (or more) good white dessert wine*
> *sprinkling of pepper*
> *kirsch*

FRUITS

3 apples, unpeeled but cored and
     chunked
1 banana, chunked
1 orange, in sections
2 pears, unpeeled but cored and
     chunked (if winter, melons
     will do)

½ pineapple, peeled and chunked
optional chunks of fruit like grapes,
     avocado, strawberries, etc.

Melt fondue ingredients in top of double boiler, adding kirsch at end. Dip a piece of apple in and taste for flavor. Add more cheese and more wine if needed, or thin a little with cream cheese if desired. Cut up fruits just before serving, arranging in bowls around fondue flame or on a platter. Move hot fondue to flame and pass out forks.

SERVES 6

Note: If you add French bread and more generous amounts of fruit, this becomes a fine luncheon or light supper.

STRAWBERRIES ROMANOFF

This sumptuous but simple dessert combines three perfect ingredients— strawberries, good fresh cream, and Grand Marnier—and then simply lets them be the stars.

3 boxes strawberries
sugar to taste (preferably from
     vanilla-bean jar)
1 quart heavy whipping cream

2 teaspoons vanilla
¼ cup Grand Marnier (or more to
     taste)
mint leaves (optional)

Stem, wash, and chill strawberries, sprinkling on the barest glaze of sugar, or none at all if strawberries are very sweet. Whip cream until reasonably, but not very, stiff. Add sugar, vanilla, and Grand Marnier. Put strawberries in large dessert bowl (preferably glass), reserving 6–8. Gently add whipped cream and mix all together. Chill until serving. Just before serving, garnish top with reserved berries and a few mint leaves.

SERVES 6–8

JOAN BURNS
MACÉDOINE OF TENDER FRUITS CASSIS

The choice of good soft fruits is crucial to this dessert, and be sure to use cassis imported from Dijon, France.

2 bananas	*1 cup raspberries*
2 peaches	*½ cup blueberries*
½ cup figs	*cassis*
1 cup strawberries, sliced	*1½ cups whipped cream*

Slice bananas and peaches, mix with figs, and heap in sherbet glasses, tumbling an assortment of berries on top. Pour cassis over all and serve. Pass a bowl of whipped cream for those who favor it.

SERVES 6

Crème de cassis, incidentally, is exquisitely good with all fruits. Unlike some liqueurs, it complements and brings out the flavor of the fruit, rather than distracting the palate.

3. APPETIZERS, DIPS, AND SNACKS

A THOUSAND AND ONE ASPARAGUS TIPS

This is a flamboyantly luxurious-looking dish to serve for parties, with very simple preparation. You can even make it economical if you save the asparagus stalks to use later in a vegetable soup.

> *6 pounds asparagus, young and fresh*
> *hot cheese dip (see Index)*

Wash asparagus and cut off tips. Blanch the tips by plunging them into boiling water for precisely 1 minute. Remove at once, cover with ice, and chill.

Fan the tips in a circle on a round plate and center with a bowl of hot cheese dip. Everyone dunks his asparagus.

SERVES 8–16

AVOCADO WITH BABY LEEKS AND BACON

1 large bunch watercress   *6 tablespoons mayonnaise*
2 avocados   *8 strips crisp bacon*
4 tablespoons small leek rings

Remove stems and wash watercress thoroughly, rinsing well under running water, then sloshing in bowl of water. Pat dry in towel. Make a watercress bed on each of 4 plates. Peel and dice avocados and place on watercress. Add leek rings. Spoon on mayonnaise, then top at last moment before bringing to table with hot crisp bacon, crumbled into bits.

SERVES 4

SOUSED CAMEMBERT WITH ALMONDS

1 8-ounce round Camembert cheese
1 cup white wine (to cover)
¼ pound butter
chopped roasted almonds

Poke some holes in the Camembert crust with the tines of a fork, then soak the cheese overnight in white wine. Next day, drain, scrape off discolored portions of the crust, and mash the cheese with the butter (which has been allowed to soften at room temperature) until it's smooth and completely mixed. Chill for a few minutes, then shape into original round cheese form, and sprinkle on a coating of the chopped almonds. Put on little wooden board or platter (or return to its container if it is a pretty wooden one), and chill until ½ hour before serving. Serve with very mild crackers, stone-ground wafers, or Scandinavian flatbread. Little chunks of French bread show off the Camembert flavor, too.

SERVES 4–6

This also makes an unusual dessert. Offer it with flower-sliced apples or pear slices. (See slicing suggestions on page 167.)

LIPTOVSKY SYR
LIPTAUER CHEESE SPREAD

Especially good with wine and beer, this rich spread was the rage in the

'40s, having come our way from Yugoslavia via Vienna. It must be seasoned so that no one flavor dominates the others. Some recipes add a little beer. It keeps well in the refrigerator for several days.

4 ounces cottage cheese, processed
    in blender
½ cup sour cream
4 tablespoons soft butter
1½ tablespoons anchovies
1 teaspoon dry mustard
1 teaspoon capers, minced

1 tablespoon minced onion
1 tablespoon caraway seeds
1 tablespoon sweet Hungarian
    paprika
⅛ teaspoon salt
freshly ground pepper

Mix all together well, then pack into a crock or bowl and let ripen overnight in the refrigerator. Serve in crock, or mound on plate, surrounded by pumpernickel bread and thin rounds of cucumber.

SERVES 6

Liptauer dip is simply the above recipe with sour cream or beer stirred in to soften the mixture.

CAVIAR–CREAM CHEESE TORTE

16 ounces cream cheese
1 4-ounce jar red caviar, slightly drained
pumpernickel bread, thin-sliced (preferably the narrow party loaf)

Soften cream cheese at room temperature for 1 hour. Shape into a large flat-topped mound. Refrigerate, covered.

Before serving, spoon red caviar over top of cream cheese, letting a little drizzle down the side. Serve with pumpernickel.

SERVES 6–8

VIRGINIA GILBERT'S
SEVICHE

2 pounds halibut or other fresh
    fish
juice of 4 limes
½ pound tomatoes, peeled and
    seeded
1 small green pepper
½ cup olive oil
¼ cup chopped parsley

2–3 tablespoons wine vinegar
dash Tabasco sauce
½ teaspoon oregano
salt
pepper
6 stuffed olives and 1 avocado for
    garnish (optional)

Skin and fillet fish (or have market do it for you), then dice. Place in glass bowl, squeeze lime juice on top, tumble fish in it, and marinate for 3 hours or more, turning pieces occasionally with a wooden spoon. Fish will be opaque and snowy-white. Dice tomatoes and green pepper and add to fish with oil, parsley, vinegar, Tabasco sauce, oregano, salt, and pepper. Mix well. Chill until serving time. Garnish with olive and avocado slices. Serve on platter with crackers, or in individual sherbet cups or small stemmed glasses. This is also good the next day.

SERVES 8

For more about seviche, see Index.

KINILAU
MARINATED FISH

This is served before dinner in Hawaii, sometimes at very opulent occasions. It can also be the main part of dinner as well as the cocktail appetizer. It is most attractive served in a transparent glass bowl.

1 pound red snapper or sea bass
    fillets
1 medium onion, chopped
2 tomatoes, chopped
2 tablespoons fresh lime or lemon
    juice

2 tablespoons white-wine vinegar
½ cup soy sauce
1 teaspoon Worcestershire sauce
    (optional)

Cut fish into cubes ⅓"–½" thick. Mix in the rest of the ingredients and marinate for at least 2 hours before serving. The citric acid in the lime juice and vinegar will "cook" the fish for you. The fish fillet will change somewhat and brighten in texture and color, and the flavor will be tingling-fresh and delicious. Serve icy-cold (pop in freezer for 4 minutes) with biscuits or crackers, on small plates or in small sherbet glasses, on a bit of lettuce or just plain. Minced parsley can be added or sprinkled on top.

SERVES 4–6

VERONICA'S
MARINATED MUSHROOMS

1½ pounds small or medium fresh mushrooms, fairly uniform in size
3 tablespoons chopped green onions
3 tablespoons finely minced parsley

MARINADE

¾ cup salad oil   *pinch of dill*
¼ cup cider vinegar   *salt and pepper to taste*
1 package Good Seasons Italian mix

Wash mushrooms under running cold water quickly. Trim bottoms of caps by removing a paper-thin sliver. Dry mushrooms and put them in a covered jar with the onion, parsley, and marinade ingredients. Shake well. Refrigerate for at least 12 hours, shaking container occasionally to make sure each mushroom soaks up its share of marinade. At serving time, drain mushrooms and serve in a bowl—or a giant brandy goblet, as Veronica does—with fancy toothpicks and napkins.

SERVES 4–16

OYSTER COCKTAIL IN TOMATO CUPS

If you have no oyster shells, here is an elegant alternative, rescued from the 1930s.

4 small tomatoes for each serving, peeled
16 small raw oysters, or 1–2 larger oysters for each serving
lettuce or watercress leaves

SAUCE

1 teaspoon horseradish   *1 teaspoon Worcestershire sauce*
1 tablespoon lemon juice   *2 drops Tabasco sauce*
1 teaspoon cider vinegar   *salt, pepper, and paprika to taste*
5 drops tarragon vinegar

Dip tomatoes in boiling water for 60 seconds and they will peel effort-lessly. Hollow out seeds and part of center: finely chop pulp (about ½ cup) and set aside. Chill tomato shells. Prepare oysters (see pages 86–87 for selecting and preparing oysters). Arrange lettuce leaves or watercress on individual small plates. Combine sauce ingredients, add pulp. Just before serving, put oysters into tomato cups, cups on top of leaves. (The oysters must be *very* cold; pop them in the freezer for a few minutes before you put them in the tomatoes.) Cover generously with sauce.

SERVES 4

SALSA FRIA
SPICY COLD TOMATO SAUCE

Less famous than the taco, but far more elegant and just as addictive, is the famed salsa fria of Mexico.

You mash it up and let it sit, then serve with tortilla chips, or dip hot meat or cheese tidbits into it. No matter what you try it with, short of Twinkies, it is maddeningly good, and terrific with cocktails, especially margaritas and daiquiris (yes, daiquiris).

4 *large ripe tomatoes, peeled (not*
    seeded) and chopped
2 *small green tomatoes, peeled*
    (not seeded) and chopped
I *large sweet onion, chopped*
I *4-ounce can peeled green*
    chilies, chopped
I *clove of garlic, minced and*
    crushed

3 *tablespoons olive oil*
3 *tablespoons wine vinegar*
2 *teaspoons minced fresh or dried*
    coriander (Chinese
    parsley)
2–3 *drops or more Tabasco sauce*
    or Mexican hot sauce
salt and pepper to taste

Mash this all together and serve very, very cold.

SERVES 6–8

To add to your Mexican-raw-food mood, follow this with a seviche (see Index) first course, and serve guacamole-stuffed tomatoes (see Index) with a hot main dish. For dessert, serve fruits South Americana (see Index) or any tropical fruits.

HOMEMADE YOGURT CHEESE

This is absurdly easy to make, and has its own mild-tangy character. Part of the fun is feeling that you are making your own cheese, with very little effort.

I *cup yogurt (homemade or from store)*

Dump the yogurt into a piece of muslin or several thicknesses of cheesecloth and let it hang over your sink overnight. Go sweet or savory: Add a tablespoon of brown sugar or a little salt before you put the yogurt in the bag. Next morning you will find a white ball of tender, creamy cheese inside. Serve as a spread with crackers.

SERVES 2–4

CUCUMBERS IN LOX-CREAM

Phyllis Sokol spoons this pink-golden sauce over cucumbers and serves on chilled plates with a caper or parsley garnish.

> *16 ounces sour cream*
> *1 small jar lox (smoked salmon)*
> *¼ medium onion*
> *3–4 cucumbers, peeled, halved, and seeded*

Blend half of sour cream with lox and onion in blender (or mince with a sharp knife). Pour into bowl with rest of sour cream and gently mix together until smooth. Serve chilled, poured on half cucumbers.

SERVES 6–8

Variation: Put mixture in bowl and surround with cucumbers and zucchini, celery sticks, radishes, or other raw vegetables.

QUICK STUFFED MUSHROOMS

> *16 medium mushrooms, fresh and plump*
> *¾–1 cup stuffing—crab mixed with mayonnaise, minced mushroom*
> *stems, and a little curry would be nice, or use whatever dip or*
> *spread you have around and like*

Quickly wash mushrooms; do not soak. Remove stems, saving for other dishes if desired. Chill caps; lightly salt hollows. Stuff with dip or spread.

SERVES 2–4

CLAM AND CHEESE LOW-CALORIE DIP

This is really too good to be called low-calorie.

1 3- or 4-ounce can minced clams
    with part of juice
1 8-ounce container cottage
    cheese
⅛ teaspoon garlic salt

sprinkle of cayenne pepper
dash Worcestershire or soy sauce
    (optional)
salt to taste
white pepper

Blend all in blender, adding as much clam juice as possible without making mixture too soupy, until it is creamy-smooth. Serve with raw vegetables or chips.

SERVES 4–6

THE RAW VEGETABLE TRAY

Remember the little dish of celery, scallions, and carrot sticks? It's still there, still loved. But now it's grown to include practically every vegetable in the book, at least in *this* book.

Here are some suggested raw vegetables, with some suggested dips. All the cracker and chip dips are good with raw vegetables, though raw vegetables have a special affinity for very salty and spicy dips.

WHICH RAW VEGETABLES?

That's easy. It all depends on what's at your market. Generally speaking, the smallest and/or the youngest are good. Any signs of wilting, sagging, or drying are not good. Greens should be brilliant. Squash should be tight-skinned. String beans should be smooth and firm, cauliflower snowy-white. Vegetables for eating raw should look pretty, or look as though they'll peel pretty. Experiment. You can always cook it if you change your mind!

HOW TO STORE RAW VEGETABLES

Tonight may be the night you're longing for a nice assortment of raw vegetables, but what do you do with any leftover vegetables?

Simple: Wash, cut, and pack assortments of raw vegetables in little Baggies, tightly sealed. They'll keep crispy-fresh for an amazing number of days. Nutritionally speaking, this may not be the super-fresh ideal way, but for busy people it's sometimes the only way.

It's a lovely sensation to open the refrigerator door and see a plastic bag full of ready-to-dip vegetables. All you have to do is spend a few seconds arranging the vegetables and getting out some dip, or maybe just seasoned salt.

ONE RAW VEGETABLE

Star a single vegetable instead of an assortment sometimes. For every-night dipping, serve one raw vegetable with a dip you like. A 60-second dip like sour cream mixed with minced dried beef and sprinkled with garlic powder is great with a 1-vegetable plate of broccoli flowerets. Or how about cool cauliflowerets with a simple (but mouthwateringly good) dip of canned tomato sauce mixed with mayonnaise?

RAW VEGETABLES FOR DIPPING

While this is not a complete list, it's enough to broaden your raw-vegetable horizons. The "harder," larger vegetables like potatoes, eggplant, beets, chayote, turnips, etc., should be peeled and cut into sticks.

asparagus	*lotus root*
beets	*mushrooms*
broccoli	*onions*
cabbage, red and white	*parsley*
carrots	*parsnips*
cauliflower	*peas*
celery	*potatoes*
celery cabbage	*radishes*
chayote	*scallions*
chili peppers	*snow pea pods*
cucumber	*squash, summer (all varieties), some*
eggplant	*winter (not banana or acorn)*
endive, French and Belgian	*string beans*
fennel	*tomatoes and cherry tomatoes*
Jerusalem artichokes	*turnips*
jicama	*zucchini*

RAW-VEGETABLE CRACKERS—A FRESH IDEA

Cut cucumbers, zucchini, potatoes, yellow squash, eggplant, turnips, etc., into "cracker" rounds. Add regular crackers, heated till very crisp. Serve with any dip, or with one of the following spreads.

MASHED BACON-CAMEMBERT SPREAD

4–6 ounces Camembert, softened
4 strips crisp bacon

Mash cheese with crumbled bacon.

SERVES 4

MASHED ROQUEFORT-OLIVE CREAM CHEESE

3 parts cream cheese   *chopped fresh chives (not frozen)*
1 part Roquefort cheese   *salt to taste*
chopped ripe olives

Soften cream cheese at room temperature. Mash with softened Roquefort, using just enough to give the cheese a good Roquefort flavor. Add olives, chives, and salt.

SESAME CHEESE SPREAD

1 part sesame seeds, lightly salted and toasted
2 parts cream cheese
salt to taste

Mash all together. Sprinkle with even more sesame seeds.

HAM SPREAD

1 small can deviled ham
1 4-ounce package cream cheese
sprinkling of cayenne pepper

Mash until blended.

SERVES 4

GUACAMOLE DIP

Authentic South American guacamoles are mashes of pure avocado with variations of spices and/or hot sauces added. But since many American palates prefer the dip with a little mayonnaise added, you should experiment to discover your own favorite, adding mayonnaise or using more Tabasco or Mexican hot sauce than the recipe here.

1 large avocado, peeled and mashed

2 tablespoons onion, finely minced or grated

½–¾ teaspoon lemon or lime juice

⅛ teaspoon salt (more to taste)

3–4 drops Tabasco sauce or Mexican hot pepper sauce

1 4-ounce can green chilies, diced (optional)

grated cheese or bacon bits (optional)

2 tablespoons mayonnaise (optional)

Mash all together, cover, and chill before serving—immerse avocado pit in dip to help keep its color. Remove pit and stir dip just before serving. Garnish with grated cheese or bacon bits. One distinguished avocado expert recommends serving the dip with the following raw vegetables: jicama, turnips, green peppers, zucchini, cauliflower, or tortilla or corn chips. But don't neglect the classic raw vegetables.

SERVES 6–8

PESTO
AN ITALIAN DIP

Pesto is a famous Italian dip/sauce for pasta, made in many different variations. Rich and salty, it's a grand dip for raw vegetables. Its origin is Genoa, where the pignolia trees flourish.

1 tin anchovies
3 or more cloves garlic, minced
½ cup pine nuts (pignolias or
*   piñons) or walnuts,*
*   ground*

1 teaspoon fresh sweet basil, or ½
*   teaspoon dried basil*
1 cup grated Parmesan cheese
2 tablespoons olive oil (or enough to
*   semiliquefy dip)*

Use Italian vegetables such as zucchini, fennel (finocchio), endive, sweet onion, green and red pepper, and mushrooms for this dip. Chunks of Italian bread on toothpicks or Italian bread sticks are also a good addition.

If you don't have a mortar and pestle, use a wooden spoon to pound and crush the anchovies into a smooth paste. Then pound in the garlic, pine nuts, and basil, working and crushing to a paste. Mix in the Parmesan and some oil (a couple of tablespoons or less) and stir well until it's thin enough to dunk vegetables, but not too thin.

SERVES 3–4

Afterward, eat a few sprigs of parsley to clear the palate of all traces of garlic.

CRUDITÉS AVEC TAPENADE
RAW VEGETABLES WITH TAPENADE DRESSING

Along the Côte d'Azur in France they have a beautiful way of zapping up raw vegetables and making the whole thing quite exciting. First, they create a sharp, audacious dressing that will send chills down your palate and evoke superlatives (in French, of course). Next, they display their usual sensitivity in a choice selection of raw vegetables.

TAPENADE DRESSING

1 egg
1 teaspoon Dijon mustard
2 teaspoons lemon juice
½ cup olive oil

1 clove garlic, chopped
3 tablespoons capers, drained
1 2-ounce tin anchovy fillets, chopped
½ cup salad or vegetable oil

Whirl egg, mustard, and lemon juice in blender. Drop by drop, or in a fine stream, add olive oil until sauce acts like mayonnaise, or at least thickens. Blend in garlic, capers, and anchovy fillets. Add, as before, remaining ½ cup oil. Dip raw vegetable in to taste. Add more lemon juice if it's not outrageously nippy.

SERVES 8–12

An authentically French array of *crudités*, or raw vegetables, would include some of the following:

small Belgian endive leaves	*radishes, with leaves left on*
thick-sliced raw mushrooms	*white icicle radishes*
cucumber sticks	*baby carrots*
cherry tomatoes	*red- or green-pepper slices*

Serve on crushed ice, or chill the platter, with dip in center.

SPICY ANCHOVY MAYONNAISE DIP

Give this dip at least a day in the refrigerator to develop its spicy, salty anchovy flavor. It's a bit aggressive for most crackers, but a perfect match for crispy, cold raw vegetables.

1 2-ounce can anchovy fillets	*1 cup or less mayonnaise*
2 tablespoons finely chopped chives or green-onion tops	*salt—just a bare pinch*
1 tablespoon tarragon wine vinegar	*⅛ teaspoon white or black pepper*
½ cup or more sour cream	

Chop the anchovies chunkily enough so that the anchovy bits can be chewed. Add remaining ingredients.

This is an example of a wildly pungent dip that complements raw vegetables.

SERVES 6–12

HOT CHEESE DIP

¾ pound coarsely grated cheddar or similar hard yellow cheese
white wine
dash Worcestershire sauce
2 drops Tabasco sauce

Melt the cheese very gently in the top of a double boiler, moistening with enough white wine to keep mixture creamy as you add other ingredients. Dip a chunk of raw vegetable in, taste, and correct seasoning if desired by adding salt or pepper, thinning if necessary with milk.

This dip tastes especially good with quartered green pepper, cauliflower, eggplant, and zucchini.

SERVES 4

SWISS-CANTON DIP

Three fabled soft cheeses from the cantons of Switzerland blend their flavors in this impeccable dip.

2 parts Gruyère cheese
2 parts Emmenthal cheese
1 part Appensell cheese

Mash these cheeses together, and let them rest at room temperature to develop their full flavor. Serve with crackers and your favorite raw vegetables.

BEER AND CHEESE DIP

½ cup mild beer
4 ounces cream cheese, softened
4–5 ounces sharp strong cheddar
*   cheese, grated or diced*
1 clove garlic

2–5 drops Worcestershire sauce, to
*   taste*
salt (optional but no more than a
*   bare sprinkle)*

Pour beer into blender. Add cream cheese and blend until smooth. Then add cheddar, garlic, and a few drops Worcestershire sauce. Blend. Taste and add salt if necessary. Pour into bowl or crock, top with a few gratings of cheese, and chill. Serve with your favorite raw vegetables and English crackers. Keeps well for at least a week.

SERVES 4

Hot Cheddar Dunk

This is the same as the preceding recipe, but served in a hot pot over a flame—a nice way to serve raw vegetables on a cold night! Heat very gently, so cheese won't coagulate.

INSTANT CHIPPED BEEF-SOUR CREAM DIP

The simplest dips are often the most delicious. I tested 4 exotic dip creations one afternoon, and tossed this in just because I'm fond of chipped beef. It won.

> *1 2½-ounce jar dried chipped beef, chopped*
> *16 ounces sour cream (or more)*
> *garlic powder (optional)*

Mix half the chipped beef into the sour cream. Taste and add more if you like, along with a little garlic powder. Garnish with bits of beef. Serve at once—this doesn't keep well.

SERVES 4–8

GINGER-SOY DIP

This is excellent with raw vegetables or crackers.

> *8 ounces sour cream*
> *1–2 teaspoons grated fresh ginger root*
> *1–2 tablespoons soy sauce*

Mix together and increase ginger and soy sauce to taste. Keep leftover ginger root in your freezer for future use.

SERVES 2—4

PROTEIN FOR PEANUTS IN PEANUT SNACKS

With the prices of ordinary sources of protein escalating at our super-market daily, one appetizing way out is to eat peanuts.

We take them far too much for granted. When in fact they are a very nutritious food, loaded with protein. A mere 2 tablespoons of peanut butter contains more protein than 1 egg. Peanuts are just short of being complete in every one of the amino acids that make up protein. To maximize the protein value, eat peanuts with a complete protein food, such as a glass of milk. This way you get good-as-steak protein, for far less money.

To save more money, buy peanuts in quantity—5 or 10 pounds if you have the refrigerator space.

RAW PEANUTS IN THE SHELL

You'll develop the same passionate fondness for these as you have for the roasted kind. Expect them to be less crispy, but more flavorful in a chewy, caramely sort of way. They keep beautifully up to two years in the refrigerator and are marvelous for midnight snacks, brown-bag lunches, floating in your purse for starving moments, lurking in the glove compartment of your car. If you eat candy at the movies, switch to these, and spend the money you save on something really elegant to eat.

HOMEMADE PEANUT BUTTER

1 cup raw peanuts (roasted can be used if preferred)
1½ tablespoons peanut oil
1½ tablespoons other oil
½ teaspoon salt

Blend peanuts with peanut oil until smooth. With blender turned on, gradually add remaining oil until the peanut butter is the right consistency, adding salt slowly as you blend. This keeps in the refrigerator for a year.

YIELDS ⅔ CUP

Variation: Follow the recipe above, but roast the peanuts first: Spread them on a roasting tray, tumble in 1½ tablespoon of peanut oil, and sprinkle with salt, then bake at 350° for 20 minutes, or until lightly toasted. Then continue with blender recipe, adding remaining oil.

THE DELICIOUS WORLD OF NUTS IN THE SHELL

Come Thanksgiving, beautiful wooden bowls of mixed nuts in the shell appear everywhere. By January, they seem to have vanished. Nuts in the shell are all raw, and marvelously delicious. They are also stunningly nutritious, so why not enjoy them for the main entree at dinner sometime? Or with fresh fruit for breakfast? And above all, think of them as the instant hors d'oeuvre.

So get cracking. Explore more than just the nut world of walnuts and almonds and filberts. Find a store that specializes in nuts, and you'll find all sorts of delectable sweetmeats. Acorns. Pistachios. Soy nuts. Cashews. Hazelnuts. Raw and roasted. In and out of the shell.

PUMPKIN SEEDS—THE SEXY HORS D'OEUVRE

> Peter, Peter, pumpkin-eater,
>   Had a wife and couldn't keep her.
> Put her in a pumpkin shell,
>   And there he kept her very well.

This innocent nursery rhyme has more wisdom than you might think. It becomes positively erotic when you consider the fact that pumpkin seeds are one of the few truly sexy foods you can eat, since raw pumpkin seeds provide a dazzling variety of those nutrients that not only build health, but supply important nutrients for hormones. Pumpkin seeds happen to taste just as good as peanuts, too. In all the Ukrainian countries, in Bulgaria, and parts of Germany and many sections of the Middle East, they are a daily food that has been treasured for centuries for both utility and virility.

STORING PUMPKIN SEEDS

Some supermarkets, virtually all health food stores, and most nut shops carry pumpkin seeds. Sold roasted in jars, they are often called "pepitas." Buy pumpkin seeds in quantities of at least 2 pounds, and you'll usually save money. They'll keep in the refrigerator for weeks, in the freezer for a year.

PUMPKIN-SEED "NUTS" IN THE RAW

Serve them at cocktails, give them to children as a snack. Put them out as a cocktail or beer nut. Nibble them with wine before dinner. Pop some in your pocket to take with you. Make little packets of them for brown-bag lunches.

HOT SEASONED PUMPKIN SEEDS

raw pumpkin seeds
1 tablespoon oil for every cup of seeds
salt and garlic powder to taste

Pour seeds on foil-lined oven pan. Pour on oil and sprinkle with salt and garlic powder. Toss with a spoon until mixed. Spread seeds flat. Put in 350° preheated oven. They'll make a popping noise when they're ready, usually in about 10–15 minutes. The idea is not to roast them, just get them piping hot.

SWEET AND NUTTY SNACK MIX

¼ pound sunflower seeds, raw or
    roasted
¼ pound pumpkin seeds, raw or
    roasted
1 pound assorted nuts, raw or
    roasted

¼ cup raisins
¼ cup semisweet chocolate chips
    (or carob chips)
½ cup tiny Oriental soy crackers
    (optional)

Mix all together, adding more or less of favorites. If you are not yet accustomed to raw nuts, include some roasted.

CHESTNUTS

Chestnuts are full of surprises. Raw, they have a deliciously sweet flavor, because they're really a fruit! They are delicious eaten roasted, too, and either way, they're a smart calorie choice (6 chestnuts = 37 calories).

Years ago roasted chestnuts were sold from little street carts everywhere, baked for many a winter dish, and quite common. But then a tree blight struck the American chestnut trees, and for a time chestnuts were scarce and expensive. Today you can again acquire a passion for chestnuts, because the blighted American chestnut has been replaced by the American-grown Spanish chestnut tree and the Chinese chestnut tree, and chestnuts are again plentiful and inexpensive. Most of the chestnuts in markets now are Spanish chestnuts. *¡Olé!*

How to Peel Chestnuts
Do not parboil, since heat destroys the sweet tang. Insert a small sharp knife into the top of each chestnut and cut an "X." Then just peel away the corners of the cross.

CHESTNUTS, CELERY, AND MUSHROOMS WITH ONION DIP

Don't wait for Thanksgiving to serve this excellent appetizer.

½ pound chestnuts
1 bunch celery, cut into dipping chunks
24 small mushrooms, very fresh
onion dip (yours, or 1 8-ounce container sour cream mixed with ½
*   large grated onion, 1 teaspoon Worcestershire sauce and salt*
*   and pepper to taste)*

Peel as described above. If you are in a hurry, make an "X" with a knife on each chestnut and then let guests finish peeling themselves. Trim a thin slice from stem bottom of mushrooms, rinse quickly and chill. Slice celery. Just before serving, assemble all on platter with onion dip in a bowl.

SERVES 6–8

CHESTNUT SALAD
Toss some chestnuts in with any green salad.

AFTER THANKSGIVING
To a mixed green salad, add *cold* leftover turkey, croutons seasoned with sage, celery, onions, and a handful of quartered raw chestnuts.

4. SOUPS

AVOCADO MADRILÈNE

1 avocado
1 can consommé madrilène
¼–½ teaspoon lemon juice

a few drops Tabasco sauce
salt and white pepper to taste
4 tablespoons sour cream for garnish

Peel avocado and remove pit; whirl in blender with consommé madrilène. Add lemon juice, Tabasco sauce, salt and pepper. Taste and correct for seasoning. Chill. Chill soup plates and spoons, too. Serve with lemon wedges, and garnish with creamy blobs of sour cream.

SERVES 2

OLD-FASHIONED COUNTRY CUCUMBER SOUP WITH BUTTERMILK

2 medium cucumbers
1 quart buttermilk
1 tablespoon chopped green onion
1 teaspoon salt
¼ cup finely chopped parsley

½ teaspoon MSG
dash pepper
cucumber slices and parsley sprigs
for garnish

Pare cucumbers, scoop out seeds, and grate or put through food chopper to make 1½ cups grated cucumber. Combine with rest of ingredients except garnish and chill 4 hours. Mix just before serving, and serve in chilled cups, garnished with slices and sprigs.

SERVES 8–10

DANISH BUTTERMILK SOUP

This has to be one of the great undiscovered dishes in America. It's a sweet yet tart soup, sumptuously good and almost disgracefully easy to prepare. In Denmark they dish it up with various accompaniments like oatcakes and jams, for luncheon or dessert. It makes an elegant instant breakfast shake, too.

3 egg yolks
½ cup sugar
1 quart buttermilk
1 teaspoon vanilla
1 teaspoon or less lemon juice

½ teaspoon grated lemon rind
¼ cup or more whipped heavy cream
blanched slivered almonds for
    garnish

Beat yolks in a large bowl until thick and ribbony when you lift the beater. Beat in sugar a little at a time. Fold in buttermilk, vanilla, lemon juice, and grated lemon rind. For luncheon or dessert, serve in soup bowls that set off the creamy vanilla soup color. Top with a dollop of cream, a sprinkling of almond slivers. If desired, pass some straw-berry jam to add at will. A plate of sweet cakes or lemon wafers is also optional.

For a quick breakfast, pour into big mugs. Top with sour cream and serve with breakfast muffins or Rytak Swedish bread and cream cheese with jam—or just plain buttered toast.

SERVES 4–6

THE WORLD OF GAZPACHO

This great cold crushed-tomato soup reigns in Spain mainly in the summer, as it should everywhere. For the great gazpacho begins, always, with fine, ripe, red, tasty tomatoes. The true gazpacho, palate-shaking and chillingly delightful, is the most famous soup of the last decade, like vichyssoise in another era. But gazpacho has more "macho," because it answers our daily craving for a salady something plus our love of spicy tomato concoctions of all kinds.

To each his own, but I feel that a great gazpacho should be authentic, and should never be made with anything but fresh tomatoes. If you add canned tomato juice, the primary flavor may be of canned tomato juice. So why bother adding 15 or 20 elegant other ingredients?

An authentic gazpacho can be served cold in glasses or mugs, as well as soup bowls. Serve it at cookouts, for casual parties or very formal dinner parties. The Spanish often add their good homemade bread to gazpacho. While this is authentic, many American versions skip the bread or substitute croutons.

Tossing in unlimited quantities of assorted fresh vegetables is risky. Discretion should be used with all but the tomatoes, although the classic ingredients of cucumber, onion, and green pepper are absolutely *de rigueur* for that inimitable gazpacho flavor base.

If you tend to go on gazpacho binges, console yourself with these thoughts: It is extremely nutritious, not extravagant in season, and very low in calories. It's eating in the raw at the gourmet level.

There is an infinite number of gazpacho recipes. I've selected just three: a truly great, classic gazpacho that you can serve as a main dish as well as a soup; an elegant but simple recipe inspired by Botin, the two-hundred-year-old restaurant in Madrid; and a quick, everyday, casual gazpacho that you can serve all year round.

CLASSIC GAZPACHO

This is the one you do by hand, lovingly crushing all the fine summer vegetables with a wooden spoon into a wooden bowl, mulling the flavors with time-honored care. This is the old way in some parts of Spain and in Cuba. It's a lovely ritual. Don't rush it. Mash. Enjoy.

3 pounds ripe, red tomatoes,
   peeled, seeded, and sliced
5 tablespoons olive oil
1 clove garlic, mashed and minced
2 cucumbers, peeled, seeded, and
   chopped
½ cup minced sweet pepper, red
   or green
½ cup minced green onion
½ cup minced celery hearts
2 tablespoons minced fresh
   parsley

2 tablespoons minced fresh dill
   (optional)
2 cups clear chicken consommé or
   stock
freshly ground pepper
2–3 tablespoons lime juice, fresh
   squeezed
a dash of Tabasco sauce
salt

Dip the tomatoes into boiling water for 60 seconds and they will peel easily. Put half the olive oil in a wooden salad bowl, add garlic and tomatoes, and mash against side of bowl with the back of a wooden spoon until mixture is soupy. Mash in other ingredients one by one. At the end, taste for seasoning, adding more herbs, pepper, salt, lime juice, and/or Tabasco as desired.

Remember: Insipid hothouse tomatoes do not a memorable gazpacho make. Good ripe or very ripe tomatoes are the soul of any gazpacho.

Chill the gazpacho for several hours, and serve with an ice cube floating in each soup bowl. It is perfectly proper to serve gazpacho without further adornment, but if you wish, pass little bowls of the following, so each person can add to his gazpacho . . .

¾ cup croutons
¾ cup sour cream
¾ cup chopped cucumber
¼ cup chopped onion, mixed with a chopped hard-boiled egg

SERVES 6

GAZPACHO ANDALUZ À LA BOTIN

Andaluz, or Andalusia, is the region of Spain where gazpacho began. This blender gazpacho recipe is modeled on that served at Botin, a world-famous restaurant in Madrid, in the heart of Andalusia.

3 thin slices bread, chopped
3 very ripe tomatoes, chopped
1 cucumber, chopped
2 cloves garlic
½–1 quart ice water
3 tablespoons olive oil or salad oil
2 tablespoons wine vinegar

2 teaspoons salt
1 teaspoon ground cumin
1 small cucumber, diced
1 tomato, diced (optional)
1 red or green pepper, diced
1 cup warmed croutons

Soak the first four ingredients in ice water for half an hour before you begin blending. Then blend at high speed until smooth. (You can put this through a coarse strainer if you prefer, but it loses the hearty texture.) Add salad oil, vinegar, salt, and cumin and blend again. Remove gazpacho, taste, and adjust seasoning, adding more salt, or perhaps a dash of vinegar. Now add a little more ice water, tasting as you go. The flavor of gazpacho is very dependent on the robustness of the tomatoes. Some will take the full quart of water called for in the recipe. Some will pale in flavor, so add the water just up to the right point.

Chill the gazpacho for half an hour to overnight. At serving time, pass chilled bowls of chopped cucumber, tomato, and pepper and the croutons, and let each person help himself.

SERVES 6

INSTANT WINTER GAZPACHO BY JOAN

There is not enough time in the world to prepare all the gazpacho that gazpacho lovers crave. This gazpacho is different. In the first place, it's really, really fast. And second, though not quite as spicy or as inspired as the Great Gazpachos, it is good. And you can have it all year round.

1 green pepper (optional)
1 onion
1 stalk celery
1 cucumber
1 large can tomato juice (the giant can)

dash Tabasco sauce
pepper
salt
1–2 ½ tablespoons safflower oil or salad oil
garlic clove

Seed pepper, peel onion, trim celery, pare cucumber, chunk all, and toss in blender with some of tomato juice. Blend thoroughly, pour into bowl, stir in rest of tomato juice and add rest of ingredients. Chill for at least an hour before serving, or refrigerate overnight. Serve in glasses, as a drink, or in soup bowls. Garnish if you wish with croutons, chopped onion, chopped hard-cooked egg, and/or chopped celery.

SERVES 10

MAST
IRANIAN CUCUMBER SOUP

This is a cool, tangy summer soup in Iran, a simple mix of finely chopped cucumber and yogurt, subtly spiced and properly served with currants floating in it.

½ cup currants (or light golden or regular dark raisins), to be mixed in or passed at table
1 ½ cups peeled, seeded, and very finely chopped cucumber
2 cups plain yogurt
1 clove garlic, crushed
1 teaspoon or more minced, crushed fresh dill (or ¼ teaspoon crushed dried dill)

½ cup cold water (just enough to liquefy)
salt to taste
2 tablespoons minced chives or green-onion tops, to be mixed in or passed at table
dash of lemon or vinegar (optional)
chopped mint leaves and/or 1 teaspoon grated lemon peel for garnish (optional)

Soak raisins or currants overnight. Stir all desired ingredients together at least an hour before serving, and let stand in refrigerator to blend flavors.

Go easy on the lemon or vinegar seasoning, because plain yogurt has a lemony tang. Eastern recipes often are altogether too lemony for some American palates. As a first course, serve small helpings—in cups rather than bowls. Pass the currants and chopped onion, so that you and your family or guests can experiment.

SERVES 2–4

This also makes a refreshing main course when served in generous soup bowls, accompanied by hot breads, warmed pita bread, or crisp breads. Pass a plate of sliced tomatoes and black olives with a little cold sliced meat, and you have quite a spread. Plan on 1½–2 cups soup per person. Or serve with *tomatesov salata* (see Index).

BLENDER TURKISH CUCUMBER SOUP
Use the preceding recipe with mint leaves, omitting currants and water. Whirl all except cucumbers in blender for 1 minute. Add cucumbers and blend 5–15 seconds, only until cucumbers are of grated consistency. Taste and add more salt, or dash of lemon. Chill 2–4 hours. Garnish with mint or onion.

SERVES 2–4

INSTANT CREAM OF TOMATO BISQUE

3 tomatoes	salt to taste
1 clove garlic	white pepper
1 teaspoon dried basil (or 3 tea-	1 cup light cream (or rich milk)
spoons chopped fresh)	½–1 cup tomato juice
¼ small onion	sour cream

Whirl tomatoes, garlic, basil, onion, salt, and pepper in blender. Strain through coarse strainer. Stir in cream and tomato juice. Chill for at least 1 hour. Taste for seasoning. Serve in chilled soup bowls with a dollop of sour cream, garnished with basil.

SERVES 2–4

5. MEATS AND SEAFOOD

BEEF

STEAK TARTARE

Legend has it that in those ancient days when nomadic tribes roamed and reigned in Europe and Asia, a young man of the Tartar tribes in search of a bride quite possibly acquired her from a distant tribe. He would ride across the hills and mountains, sweep down upon a woman who caught his eye, steal her, ravish her, and claim her for his own. Certainly Genghis Khan procured a bride in this manner: as a matter of fact, she happened to belong to another man.

Legend also has it that the marauding suitor carried a slab of raw beef under his saddle, which, devoured just before reaching his destination, gave him sudden strength for the capture. Crushed between the saddle and the horse during a long gallop, the steak was incredibly tender and delicious.

Thus raw steak began a long, glorious trek down through history, as "steak tartare." With a story like that behind it, its reputation as a virility food has endured.

Each country, each city, and sometimes each restaurant and household has devised delicious variations of steak tartare, but the base is always very fresh, and freshly ground or minced, very lean beef. In Scandinavia it is presented with a gleaming egg yolk in the center. In Ethiopia, with an excruciatingly hot berbere sauce. In France, fluffed with a gossamer mixture of oils and spices. And so on . . .

How to Select the Steak

Steak tartare is delicious made with several different cuts of beef. The most elegant are filet mignon, New York cut filets, tournedo filets from the whole filet mignon, top round, and top sirloin. By far the most popular are the top round and top sirloin. Both provide reasonably priced cuts with luxury flavor.

Steak tartare is meant to be eaten raw, and therefore it must be immaculately clean and fresh. You should purchase steak-tartare beef only from a butcher or a market you respect. Shop in a good store and dine within a few hours to be assured fresh, sumptuously good flavor. Do not purchase meat that has been prepackaged, no matter how elegant a cut, and don't let it stay in the refrigerator overnight. Tell the butcher you're going to eat the meat raw and remind him to cut or grind it on equipment that has not been used for pork—and watch him do it. Some people prefer to grind or mince or scrape their meat at home, to eliminate any possibility of contracting trichinosis from pork products. The possibility is remote, but it exists, so why not be careful?

CLASSIC STEAK TARTARE WITH ANCHOVIES

This has to be one of the most satisfying of all eating experiences. This recipe has the traditional tartare ingredients found in French, Austrian, and German recipes, with an American flavor, and is rather easy to put together.

1½ pounds top round or top
    sirloin, chopped finely or
    ground
2 egg yolks
1 tablespoon olive oil
½ tablespoon vinegar
2 tablespoons capers
2 tablespoons minced onion
10 anchovies (rolled anchovies
    with capers or flat fillets
    may be used), cut into 4
    or 5 bits each

1 tablespoon Grey Poupon
    mustard
⅛ teaspoon salt
⅛ teaspoon freshly ground
    pepper
parsley and more minced onion
    for garnish

Place chilled ground steak on a platter, flatten, and make a deep well in the center. Into this put egg yolks and liquid ingredients, then rest of ingredients (except garnish) and mix very lightly (fluff it, don't crush it) with two forks. The trick is to blend the dressing and seasonings, but not too much, since you want to be able to savor the different flavors of the tender beef, the savory anchovy bits, and so on. Serve garnished with parsley and onion, with a very good French or pumpernickel bread, some sliced tomatoes, black olives, and perhaps a light salad.

SERVES 4

STEAK TARTARE DINNER, FAMILY STYLE

This is the way children often prefer it, and the way dieters adore it. It's almost as good as the fancy steak tartares, and exquisitely satisfying in its own purist way.

This is our family's "vacation" tartare. We pack along the capers, etc., in the car and stop at markets to pick up the meat for an impromptu picnic supper at our overnight stop. A loaf of bread, tomatoes, and fruit round out the meal.

*1¼ pound round steak or sirloin tip, fat removed, ground while you
    watch or minced yourself (see page 65)*
*raw vegetables, a few tomato slices, 1–2 tablespoons chopped onion,
    and a few capers for each serving as garnish*

Chill meat until serving. At serving time (within a few hours), put a
portion of meat on each plate. Mash with fork in crisscross pattern to
give it a nicely textured surface, and sprinkle on garnish. Big sliced
tomatoes and delicatessen salads are great with this, too.

SERVES 4

CAVIAR–STEAK TARTARE SANDWICH

4 slices rye bread
4 tablespoons unsalted butter
*½ pound raw scraped or twice-
    ground fresh beef*
1 large onion, finely minced
*4 tablespoons Danish/Scandina-
    vian caviar (lumpfish roe)*

*1 tablespoon grated fresh or
    frozen horseradish*
1 hard-cooked egg, chopped
2 tablespoons capers (optional)

Butter rye bread right to edges to keep it from getting soggy. Top with
a layer ¼"–1" thick of meat. Border edges with minced onion. With
a spoon, make a hollow in center of meat and fill with 1 or more teaspoons of Danish caviar. Sprinkle very sparingly with horseradish (it's
strong!), chopped egg, and a few capers.

Properly speaking, this is part of an assortment of Danish open
sandwiches for appetizers known as smorrebrod, but it's also a meal
within itself that puts the sandwich into very elegant territory.

SERVES 2–4

HAM

RAW-CURED HAM AND PROSCIUTTO

Many of the most famous hams in the world are referred to as "raw." In fact, they are neither raw nor cooked, but are preserved by curing.

Curing is a far-flung industry, practiced, in some cases, according to centuries-old traditions of fine flavor. It involves salting, air-drying, smoking, pickling, brining, dry-salting, or a combination of these processes. The results are highly individual flavor of consummate perfection.

The Jambons de Bayonne of France, the cured Westphalian ham of Germany, the Prague ham of Czechoslovakia, some York hams of England, and the prosciutto of Italy are world-famous examples. Prosciutto is the best-known cured ham in the United States, readily available at Italian and gourmet markets, but you should search for and sample some of these other great cured hams, too, all of which deserve their noble reputations, and can be used in prosciutto recipes with interchangeable ease. Inquire locally at the better meat markets.

Remember, they need no cooking, no seasoning, no fussing. You just eat them. In their raw-cured state, they are perfect.

PROSCIUTTO WITH MELON

This is nice for casual get-togethers, family suppers, or as part of a sumptuous formal party. With soup, marinated mushrooms (see Index), an Italian chicory salad (see Index), and fresh-baked bread, it's a feast.

> *1 cantaloupe*
> *¼ pound prosciutto, sliced paper-thin*

Peel, seed, and cut up cantaloupe into bite-size pieces approximately 2" long and ¾" through the middle. Wrap a small piece of prosciutto around each piece and spear through with toothpick to hold it wrapped. Prosciutto has a powerful flavor, and you don't want to use too much on each slice of fruit, so wrap sparingly—just enough to go around and overlap enough to put toothpick through. Set out on platter and serve chilled. The wine-red of the ham and the pale orange of cantaloupe make for a sparkling visual and gastronomic treat.

SERVES 4–8

PROSCIUTTO, BREAD, AND HONEY

Caesar Augustus could have eaten this meal, adding a few olives and figs, a bunch of grapes, and a glass of wine for a light luncheon. For an evening meal, add a hearty salad course such as avocado and grapefruit salad, peeled cherry tomato salad, or watercress salad with walnuts and turkey (see Index for all).

> *Italian bread in thin slices*
> *honey*
> *⅛ pound prosciutto per person*

Spread each slice of bread lightly with honey and top with a slice of prosciutto.

LAMB

In Lebanon they make a version of steak tartare with lamb: kibbeh. It's kneaded raw with a very good cracked wheat called bulghur and served as an hors d'oeuvre, a dinner course, or the main entree for less elaborate dinners. Traditionally it is scooped onto little slices of pita bread or unleavened breads, and it is a great favorite. Along with a number of other Middle Eastern dishes, kibbeh has experienced a rise in popularity with Americans recently. It's quite simple to prepare, but there is a ritual which you must follow closely.

KIBBEH
THE BUSTANY FAMILY RECIPE

Get into your Middle Eastern mood, light some candles, and serve this traditional raw-lamb dish.

2 handfuls (not too much, it expands) of medium (not fine) bulghur
1 cup water
1 pound very lean, fresh, twice-ground leg of lamb (tell the butcher it is for a dish eaten raw, so grinder must be very clean, and ask him to grind it twice for you)

½ onion, chopped very fine or ground with meat
⅛ teaspoon cumin (6 or 7 generous shakes from container)
salt and pepper to taste
⅛ cup or less olive oil

In the morning, or 4–7 hours before serving, rinse cracked wheat well, then soak in 1 cup water a few minutes. Squeeze very dry in towel. Grind the lamb twice if your butcher didn't do it for you. Combine lamb and wheat and start kneading, adding onion, cumin, salt, and a little pepper. For easy kneading, moisten your hands on a couple of ice cubes. Knead for 3 minutes. Taste for seasoning, being careful not to oversalt. Form into patties, glaze with a drizzling of olive oil, cover, and chill for at least 4 hours so the lamb, wheat, and onion flavors can subtly merge. Serve sprinkled with a little salt, a little more olive oil if preferred. Each person scoops the kibbeh onto pieces of fresh pita or unleavened bread.

SERVES 4

Note: Nice for dinner, Eastern fashion, with breads and a salad. Try an Armenian *tomatesov salata* (see Index) with a tall glass of tan (half yogurt, half ice water), or tabouli (see Index). Or your own favorite green salad.

CHI KUFTA
STEAK TARTARE, ARMENIAN STYLE

¾ cup fine bulghur
½ cup cold water
1 pound very lean, very fresh leg of
    lamb, ground twice by the
    butcher (or you) in a clean
    grinder

salt and pepper to taste
1 pinch cayenne pepper
1 medium onion, finely minced
1 cup parsley, finely minced
minced scallions for garnish

Combine bulghur and water; let stand for ½ hour and squeeze thoroughly dry. Add meat and seasonings and knead the mixture like dough. Moisten your hands with cold water occasionally as you knead the mixture. Add the onion and 1 heaping tablespoon of parsley and knead again. After kneading for a total of 10 *minutes* (yes, isn't that bizarre?), taste a bit of the kufta to make sure bulghur is no longer crunchy, and has blended. Shape into small patties on platter. Garnish liberally with remaining parsley and scallions and serve at once.

SERVES 4–6 AS ENTREE, 10–12 AS APPETIZER

Note: Should you have leftovers, they make lovely broiled meat patties for another time, and freeze well.

FRESH FISH FROM THE SEA

Each island, each shore, each country yields it own bounty of fresh fish, and has its own ways with raw-fish dishes. Those who catch the fish know well how beautiful and how immaculately clean most fresh fish is. And how good it tastes, not cooked, but served in a small sea of tangy marinades and sauces, or preserved with fresh herbs, or flavored in delicate brines.

In almost every country of Central and South America, and in Mexico, seviche—raw fish marinated in lime juice—is a favorite food. From another part of the world, the South Pacific, comes another exotic series of raw-fish dishes: kinilau and lomi lomi salmon from Hawaii, for instance.

Two continents away, in Scandinavia, the majestic gravlax—marinated fresh salmon—reigns supreme.

It is in Japan that fresh raw fish reaches a pinnacle in the national cuisine. Served as sashimi and in sushi, it becomes a high gourmet art. For in Japan, the subtle nuances of working with the most natural of foods have been raised to a sophisticated perfection. Cooking is done with an extraordinarily light touch, and even the arranging of food is an advanced form of creative artistry. The Japanese have a highly civilized awareness of, and respect for, the natural perfection of raw foods.

How to Select Fish

To get fresh fish these days, it isn't necessary to live near the sea. Japanese and gourmet markets are ideal sources, and most cities and towns have market chains that fly in very fresh fish on certain occasions and during some fishing seasons. Salmon, for example, fresh and appetizing, when plentiful is flown throughout the country by big supermarket chains. Eastern oysters are flown west. Hawaiian tuna, prized for sashimi, is flown to many American market areas.

Talk to the fish buyers at your market. Tell them you are not planning to cook your fish, but to marinate it raw (or, in the case of sashimi, serve it raw, dipped in a special sauce). Ocean fish is required in the United States because of pollution of fresh waters, and the salty flavor of the sea is part of the whole superb taste.

Remember, the fish cannot be prepackaged in a regular supermarket package. It must be fresh, or flash-frozen only by the highest standards.

Here are some of the fish frequently served raw:

albacore (*a tuna*)	*salmon*
flounder	*scallops*
halibut	*sea bass*
Hawaiian tuna	*sea urchins*
octopus	*shrimp* (*only in Japan*)
pompano	*tuna*
red snapper	*whitefish*

SEVICHE

From Mexico, from Central America, and from South America come an infinity of popular local recipes that have now gone international, for the basic fish-in-lime-or-lemon-juice dish that is most often called seviche (also spelled ceviche in some regions).

Seviche, although not cooked, is not exactly raw. As it marinates in lime juice, citric acid in the juice actually "cooks" the fish, changing it from translucent to opaque and giving it a succulent, tender chewiness a bit like very tender chicken.

Recipes range from the simplest fisherman's stir-together lunch at sea to the most elaborate and sophisticated party seviches (see Index). Very often the amounts of tomato and pepper and parsley and onion that are included will depend on your own personal palate and on what is cheap and available. No matter what you mix in, it always seems to taste great.

SIMPLE SEVICHE FOR ONE

A good thought for single eaters: Toss fish in lime juice in the morning, and dinner is ready when you get home, waiting in the refrigerator. Multiply by two or three and you have enough for dinner guests.

3–5 ounces fresh fish fillets or
*   scallops*
juice of 1 lemon (or lime)
juice of 1 lime
dash angostura bitters

2 tablespoons chopped goodies,
*   like onions, tomato, green*
*   pepper, whatever is*
*   around*

Cut fish into bite-size pieces and immerse in juices in covered dish in refrigerator. A few hours later, or after work, add condiments and let sit for another hour or more. Good with crackers or bread. Pretty on a lettuce leaf. Taste and add salt and/or pepper before serving. Serve with a mug of gazpacho (see Index) or avocado madrilène (see Index) and a hot boiled potato.

SERVES 1

SEVICHE INSPIRED BY SR. PICO

1½ pounds corvina, sea bass, red
*   snapper*
juice of 6 limes
1½ teaspoons sugar

2 teaspoons salt
1½ teaspoons pepper
6 dashes hot pepper
3 cups chopped peeled tomatoes

Cut very fresh raw fish fillets (see shopping directions on pages 72–73) into bite-size pieces. Marinate in lime juice for 3 hours. Stir in other ingredients, and some minced parsley and onion, perhaps, just before serving. Taste and adjust seasoning if necessary. Pass hot pepper at the table for fiery-food buffs.

SERVES 4–6

SASHIMI

The essence of sashimi, the famous gourmet dish from Japan, is its simplicity. It is really only a deft revelation of one of nature's most sumptuous offerings: fresh sliced seafood, dipped in a delightfully tangy sauce. The illustrious sashimi is more than just another gourmet treat: It is superbly nutritious, and offers its maximum value when served raw. Sashimi is also a highly digestible food, prized by some Japanese when convalescing. It is also low in calories. Serve sashimi with cocktails or sake as an appetizer, first course, or main entree.

1 pound fresh tuna fillets (or other fresh fish)
½ teaspoon wasabi paste (horseradish powder mixed with a little water)
¾ cup soy sauce

grated white daikon radish (optional)
decorative greens (6–8 sprigs parsley, or some curly lettuce)

Have the market skin and fillet the fish, reminding them that you are serving it raw as sashimi. While Oriental markets are the best sources, since they serve a sashimi- and sushi-sophisticated clientele, any quality fish market is fine.

Take fish home, chill, and serve that afternoon or evening. If it's tuna, don't expect the look of canned tuna; it will be a handsome deep wine-red fillet. Shortly before serving, mix some pale-green wasabi horseradish powder (available in cans from regular markets or Oriental stores) with a little water until it forms a solid paste. Serve on a plate, or wooden board, and put dab of wasabi in one corner. Decorate with a bit of parsley, a small chrysanthemum-cut raw turnip or daikon radish. Slice tuna fillet crosswise on a slight slant into bite-size pieces ¼" thick, 1"–2" long. Pour soy sauce into dipping dish, furnish forks or chopsticks, and little napkins, and serve.

Each person helps himself, dipping each bite of sashimi into a bit of the wasabi, then into soy sauce, or even eating fish plain. If you like, you can stir the wasabi into the soy sauce to create a dipping sauce of the exact hotness you want.

SERVES 3–4 AS ENTREE, 6–8 AS APPETIZER

Variations: If you like ginger, you'll adore this. Prepare as above but add freshly grated ginger root to the soy sauce, to make a ginger-and-soy dip. The wasabi horseradish powder can be included or dispensed with. Fresh ginger root is easily stored in your freezer. Grate it, frozen, right into sauce.

HERE IS HOW YOUR SASHIMI PLATE MIGHT LOOK

If you want to serve a more assorted sashimi, consult the market on the very fresh fish fillets available for each season and locality. You might also include octopus (which is often blanched briefly by the market) and squid, or sea-urchin roe. Cooked crab and lobster are colorful additions to a sashimi array, but are definitely optional. See the fish list on page 73. Allow ⅛ pound fish per person for appetizers, ¼ pound per person for dinner entrees.

A popular sushi is served topped with delicate, gleaming sea-urchin roe.

SERVING FROZEN SASHIMI

While sashimi is at its most superb with fresh seafood, frozen fish may be used if it is the finest of fish, frozen under the most stringent of special conditions. Purchase it only at a Japanese market that caters to a raw-fish-eating clientele, or a fish market of exemplary quality. Frozen scallops, for example, are delicious. There is a little moisture loss on defrosting.

SUSHI

Sushi, while related to sashimi, is different in that it consists of raw fish served on seasoned rice. Although Japanese sushi-makers practice an art of graceful ritualized movement in the preparation of sushi, it is actually a very simple making-mudpies type of operation, and lots of fun to do. The result is an exquisitely delicate and fresh appetizer—or, if you want to keep on going, as most do, a meal to remember.

Like sashimi, sushi can be made with just one kind of fish fillet or with many. It's basically a pressed chunk of cooked spiced rice served warm or cold with raw fish on top.

1½ pounds raw fish fillets (tuna or assorted), cut into pieces to fit on top of sushi rice ovals
wasabi horseradish powder, mixed into a paste with water
soy sauce
bits of dried seaweed or radish, for garnish

RICE

3¼ cups water	*1½ teaspoons salt*
a small piece of kombu kelp, if available	*4 tablespoons sugar (or*
3 cups rice, rinsed and drained	*less)*
⅓ cup sweet Japanese rice vinegar	*1 teaspoon MSG (optional)*

A sushi bar is a good place to get ideas on the variations of sushi. Sushi is like canapés—it's tempting to do them up in different ways. Example: First you crisscross 2 fish slices, then you put on a bit of shredded daikon radish or dried seaweed, etc.

To make the rice, boil water, adding kombu kelp if used. Add rice and heat to a boil. Remove kombu, cover pan tightly, and simmer the rice 15 minutes, or until tender. While it's boiling, mix vinegar with salt, sugar, and MSG. Turn rice out into a pan. Sprinkle with vinegar mix and stir. Refrigerate. Make rice layer shallow so it will cool rapidly. You will have about 6 cups rice, for about 36 sushi.

In sushi bars, as in many Japanese homes, the rice is elegantly pressed in a compartmented wooden tray that is halved, filled, then pushed together. Handmade sushi is also traditional. In the palm of your hand, make an oval of rice not longer than 2" and less than ½" deep. Press it into an oval shape by pushing quite firmly with your palms cupped together. Your sushi pieces should be like oval bases, or "crackers."

At serving time, in the kitchen or at the table, sushi-bar style, brush or dab a little wasabi on each oval of rice. That's all! Arrange on a plate or board, garnish, and serve with soy sauce.

SERVES 4–6

NORIMAKI SUSHI

Same as above, but with the addition of nori, a seaweed that comes packaged in crispy sheets. Spread rice on a sheet of nori, brush with wasabi and soy sauce, then place fish and slivers of cucumber across the middle. Roll up like a jellyroll, and cut crosswise in 1"–2" pieces. Fun!

SALMON

When the water reached the top of his sealskin boots, he stopped and stood quietly, his eyes adjusting to the strong sunlight that flashed across the water. . . . Then he struck downward with a thrust so swift that I could not see it, and when he raised the spear again, it held a huge thrashing sea trout [salmon]. . . . Then everyone seemed to have a shining sea trout. . . . The women and children leaped back, laughing, then lunged at the big cold slippery fish. . . . When anyone on the bank caught hold of

one . . . they carried it back to the hollow stone cairn, where the
fish lay in a mounting pile of shining silver. . . . That evening
we slit open and ate the beautiful cold pink flesh on the sea trout
until we were filled and could eat no more.

—JAMES HOUSTON, *The White Dawn*

Salmon springs from the sea looking not raw at all, but pink, gleaming, and perfect. Since its raw elegance is so appealing, it has spawned
a beautiful variety of gourmet dishes in many countries, over many
centuries.

All of the salmon recipes here, from the South Seas, from Hawaii,
from Scandinavia, are authentic gourmet dishes. They are among the
Beautiful Dishes served to heads of state, the impossibly rich and
famous everywhere, and all who are well-traveled in the world of food.

GRAVLAX (SWEDISH MARINATED SALMON)

In Norway they call it gravlaks. In some parts of Scandinavia, gravad
lax. In America, as gravlax, it is renowned as an absolutely superb way
to prepare fresh salmon in season. How does it taste? Heavenly. It is
actually simply home-cured fresh salmon, marinated in the fragrance
of fresh dill with salt and spice. Serve with iced butter, on bits of dark-
brown bread at cocktail time. Or with chilled bottles of fine imported
beer. Or slice on dinner plates with wedges of lemon and feathery
sprigs of fragrant fresh dill, accompanied by steaming boiled new
potatoes. And since you have cured your salmon in salt, it keeps very
well in the refrigerator for many days. If you catch your own salmon,
do make your own gravlax. Fresh dill is crucial to the flavor. And fresh
(not packaged) salmon, from a good market.

GRAVLAX DINNER WITH MUSTARD DRESSING

Gravlax is a very satisfying dinner. Fan out some slices on each plate,
with a wedge of lemon and good hot steamed or boiled potatoes. Pass

the mustard sauce. And serve your salad *after* this gravlax main course, European style. Cucumber or endive salad would be a natural. And perhaps gazpacho (see Index) to start with.

> *3 pounds fresh center-cut salmon*
> *1–2 bunches fresh dill (to make 2 cups or more coarsely cut)*
> *1½ tablespoons crushed peppercorns*
> *⅓ cup sugar*
> *¼ cup salt*

MUSTARD DRESSING

3 tablespoons olive oil or other salad oil	*salt and pepper*
1½ teaspoons wine vinegar	*1 teaspoon or more sugar*
1 teaspoon or more rich Swedish or Dijon-type mustard	*chopped dill*

Ask your fish-market man to split and fillet lengthwise a very fresh whole salmon for you, or order a piece of center-cut salmon, filleted in half. As you prefer, serve with or without the skin.

Wash, dry, and blot dill on a paper towel and cut coarsely. Mix crushed peppercorns with sugar and salt. Bring out a long, low dish that will hold the salmon. Sprinkle the bottom with some of the dill. Put in one salmon fillet, silver-skin side down, after rubbing it with the salt-sugar-pepper mixture. Put the rest of dill evenly all over the top of the fillet, sprinkle lots of the seasoning mixture evenly about, and top with second half of the fillet, skin-side up. You have now made a sandwich between two slices of salmon. Lay the last of the dill on top and follow with a last little sprinkle of the salt mixture. Cover with plastic wrap or foil. Weigh down the salmon with a plate and some object—a book will do—weighing 3–4 pounds. Salmon must be pressed in this manner to marinate evenly. Refrigerate. Marinate for 48 hours to 3 days. Every 12 hours, remove from refrigerator and baste the salmon with the natural juices in the dish, inside and out. Turn the whole fillet over once during refrigeration.

When you're ready to serve, combine the mustard-dressing ingredients and stir until smooth. The mustard flavor should be very vibrant. Remove salmon and brush off all the salt, dill, and pepper with a damp clean cloth. With a very sharp knife, cut thin slices down to, but not through, the silver skin, and gently cut away from skin. Arrange on handsome wooden board or platter, garnished with lemon wedges, and a bit of parsley. Serve the thinly sliced salmon, accompanied by mustard dressing, with very thinly sliced dark bread and a crock of unsalted butter. (Some prefer it with no butter at all.) And enjoy!

SERVES 8–10 AS ENTREE, 12–20 AS APPETIZER

Note: After being removed from marinade, gravlax will keep nicely, covered, in the refrigerator for several days. The mustard dressing is excellent with other cold foods, both meat and fish.

SALMON AND YOGURT

sea salt to taste
¼ cup lemon juice
chopped fresh dill, or crushed dill seeds
¾ pound fresh salmon, sliced

½ onion, sliced thin
¼ onion, chopped
1 8-ounce container yogurt (or sour cream)

Make a dressing of the salt, lemon juice, and dill. Combine in a jar or bowl with the salmon and sliced onion. Allow to marinate for several hours. Drain. Add more salt and pepper to taste. Just before serving, fold in yogurt and mix so that all ingredients are covered with yogurt. Garnish with chopped onion. Serve with tomato wedges, sliced cucumbers, and hot boiled potatoes tumbled in butter and parsley.

SERVES 2

LOMI LOMI SALMON

Lomi Lomi salmon is the Hawaiian version of seviche, and, like seviche, the fish is marinated in lime juice, which actually "cooks" the fish. The fillets change color, and take on the texture of tender cooked fish. Leftovers just marinate another day, and taste deliciously fresh. This is good on crackers.

1 ½ pounds fresh salmon fillets   *pepper*
juice of 3 limes   *dash Tabasco sauce*
4 ripe tomatoes, peeled and diced   *2 teaspoons salad oil*
½ cup chopped scallions   *lettuce leaves*
salt   *1 lime for garnish*

Cut salmon fillets into long narrow strips. Put salmon in a glass or earthenware bowl, add lime juice, and cover. Chill for several hours. Drain salmon and rinse with very cold water. Mix salmon with tomatoes and scallions. Season to taste with salt, pepper, oil, and Tabasco sauce. It should be spicy. Chill until very cold. Serve spooned onto lettuce leaves, garnished with lime slices. Serve as buffet, hors d'oeuvre, or main dish. A Hawaiian fruit dessert would be pleasant.

SERVES 6 AS ENTREE, 10–16 AS APPETIZER

BIVALVES: GOURMET CLASSICS OF THE SEA

Close to the shores of countries all over the earth live a particularly flavorful group of sea creatures known as bivalves. They all have one, or rather two, things in common: Two shells get together to provide an open-and-shut case for raw-food gourmet eating.

We're including here clams, oysters, and scallops. If you dine on these luscious bivalves, you must be aware of certain rules. Your shopping must be done at reputable fish markets, and this applies whether you live by the sea or inland. If you do your own foraging, you must consult regionally with your Fish and Game Department. When bivalves are out of season, hunting is not only illegal, it's unsafe. Check, too, on any chance of pollution in shore waters of your region. Shop at specialty markets (Oriental and fine-fish markets). Find out what's available when, and then you can relax and relish these famous foods.

RAW CLAMS

> First catch your clams; along the
>   webbing edges
> of saline coves you'll find
>   the precious wedges.
>
>   17th century English anonymous

People who love raw clams behave in a manner that is comprehensible only to other people who love raw clams. They pant with anticipation, moan with delight, and in general resemble rock singers in mid-concert. There is no way to describe the taste; it's an individual and very sensual experience. Some people chew them. Some people just sort of gently let them slide down. Nobody is really quite clear on the subject.

Clams are surprisingly available, as they are flown from New England and Japan and Florida all over the United States. Buy only the small clams, about 1"–2½" across; big clams are delicious but tougher, and usually need to be cooked. Wash clams and scrub the shells under cold running water. Refrigerate them if you need to, but no more than 24 hours. Just before serving, take a small, straight, sturdy, sharp knife (or, of course, a clam knife) and insert the knife in the lip of the clam, at the part near the hinge (the fat back part of clam). Work the knife into the lip until it's well inserted. Now pry the clam open by holding the clam firmly and tilting the knife. Throw away clams that open themselves; they are not fresh.

Cherrystone and littleneck clams are great favorites. But all small clams are delicious raw. For beauty and convenience, they are always served on the half shell.

CHERRYSTONE CLAMS ON THE HALF SHELL WITH
SPICY COCKTAIL SAUCE

8–16 clams per person

SPICY COCKTAIL SAUCE

1 cup ketchup

1 tablespoon lemon juice

1 teaspoon onion juice or grated
   raw onion

1/4 teaspoon Worcestershire sauce

few drops Tabasco sauce (more if
   you like hotter sauce)

1 tablespoon sugar

1 tablespoon prepared horseradish

1/2 teaspoon salt

1/4 teaspoon MSG (optional)

Mix the sauce ingredients thoroughly, chill to blend flavors, taste and adjust seasoning. Put tiny bowls of cocktail sauce in the center of each plate. Surround with clams, opened, on the half shell. (On a bed of crushed ice is lovely.) Wedges of lemon and a sprig of parsley are nice but not necessary. Small-pronged clam or cocktail forks are used to pick the clam from its shell. The clam is dipped in the sauce and then —ecstasy! It is consumed.

THE SENSUAL OYSTER

Oysters are like champagne. The meal at which they are served becomes an event, rather than just another occasion. They definitely create a gala atmosphere, and people tend to wax ecstatic and emotional over them. The myth that they contain an aphrodisiac is, however (alas!), a myth. But insofar as good nutrition makes your lust for life increase— yes, they are sexy. And since eating raw oysters is indeed a sensual experience, they continue to be written up as seduction foods.

There have been songs sung about the oyster, books written, stories told down through the centuries since man first stumbled upon this delicate morsel. And it was *early* man, for, as we well know from fossil remains at ancient campsites, oysters have been a favorite for millennia.

The oyster is more than delicious, it is ecologically important. It thrives along shallow coastal waters, fastening on to coastal rocks and gobbling prodigious quantities of sea water each day of its existence.

As the oyster's food is the organic material washed down from the adjacent shores, the oyster is perhaps the first to know when the water is polluted. It promptly begins to fade away, and thus has become one of our primary early-warning systems about pollution.

Oysters, once so plentiful and cheap that they sustained the poorest man, have now become rarer, and an expensive delicacy for many, as oyster beds have been depleted by overharvesting and by pollution. Many a bed is gone forever. But many another oyster bed is now being treated with care. Oysters, which have been imported and planted with great success in some areas, are now being farmed. And the dangers of sea-water pollution from industry and from land runoffs and sewage are at least being publicized. Hopefully, the public everywhere will react aggressively. Where water pollution threatens oysters, it will ultimately threaten people.

What is the oyster? It is a bivalve mollusk that grows in a distinctively wavy, ribbony shell that is of extraordinarily pretty design. Attached to its rocky bed, it attracts bits of seaweed and an occasional barnacle until it looks vaguely like the rocks it grows upon. Most oysters are revealed on their rocky beds only at minus tides, which occur every few months. Within this shell, which opens from a single small hinge, in bivalve fashion, like a clam, lies the divine oyster. Pale and shimmering, softly beige, ringed with a brown frill at the edges, decorated with a deep-beige dot at one end (the muscle that attaches it to the shell), the oyster is ready to eat just as nature has prepared it. The inside of the shell is pearly and perfect, immaculately fresh and clean and smooth, except for a tiny line of small half moons that look like a designer signature, indented like a bas-relief against the pearly smoothness.

HARVESTING YOUR OWN OYSTERS
For many people, this is an occasional seashore experience. But there are rules you must remember. You must harvest only the quantity

allowed by the local Fish and Game regulations (usually 8–16 per person). You return the empty shells to the beds. They are needed desperately because they hold the invisible, microscopic "seeds" of future oysters.

The best way to harvest an oyster is to *not* pry it away from the rock, but to open the shell right there, remove the top shell (or open wide enough), cut the muscle of the oyster, and let it slip into a plastic container. Some people bring along a jar of sauce, and have an oyster picnic on the spot. Never visit an oyster bed without checking with the local Fish and Game department or the Coast Guard, since oyster beds are unsafe at times, or out of season. Others are privately owned, or considered endangered (so no harvesting is being done at all until the bed has had a chance to insure its own survival). And, sadly, in certain urban areas near factories and sewage plants, the oysters are not harvested at all because of pollution.

BUYING OYSTERS

At fish markets you can buy fresh raw oysters right in their shells, or in a jar. Buy fresh oysters in their shells at least once, so you can save the pretty bottom shells for later use. There are different sizes and types of oysters, but medium and small are best raw. They'll keep for at least a day or two in the refrigerator.

OYSTERS ON THE HALF SHELL

4–6 oysters per person (12 if for entree)
spicy cocktail sauce (see Index) or bottled sauce
lime or lemon quarters (optional)
chilled parsley sprigs (or watercress or curly endive) for garnish

Put dinner plates in refrigerator or freezer to chill. Remove oysters from refrigerator and scrub thoroughly with stiff brush under running water. Place flat side up. Insert a small but sturdy knife blade (special oyster knives are available) between the edges of the shell opposite hinges. You will see the line where the shell meets. If you have difficulty, break off a bit of the thin shell edge, then insert knife in the revealed slit. Twist the knife and the shell will pry open quite obligingly. Slip the knife between oyster and top shell to cut the little muscle that attaches it. (Be careful, the knife can slip!) Take your time and you'll get the knack. Now twist off the top shell. The oyster lies there invitingly in its half shell. Just slip the knife under it to cut the little attachment between oyster and bottom shell, so it can be lifted from shell with a fork. Discard any oysters that open themselves but do not close. They are not fresh.

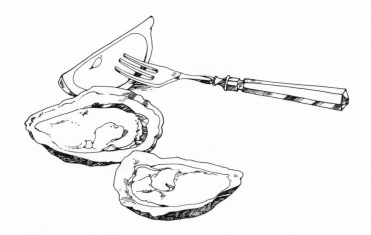

Arrange chilled oysters on the half shell on icy plates, or on a bed of crushed ice, as it's done in the best restaurants. Center with sauce in tiny bowls or paper cups. Add lime or lemon quarters and a few decorative sprigs of parsley. Serve your oysters with white wine or a noble imported beer, and big napkins, tiny forks, and French bread.

OYSTERS AND CAVIAR, VENETIAN STYLE

8 oysters
2 teaspoons lemon juice
dash cayenne pepper
2 tablespoons or more caviar

Open oysters but retain both parts of the shell. Mix lemon juice, cayenne (go lightly, it's very hot), and caviar. Spread this thinly. Close
shell, and serve on ice.

SERVES 1–4

OYSTERS IN MUSHROOM CAPS

A delightful way to serve smaller oysters.

12 medium mushroom caps, very fresh
¾ cup oil-and-vinegar dressing
spicy cocktail sauce (see Index) or your own favorite sauce
12 small Olympia or Eastern fresh raw oysters

Marinate the mushroom caps in the oil-and-vinegar dressing for 8–24
hours. (Save dressing to use later as a regular salad dressing.) Mix
sauce. Chill oysters, having bought them very fresh that very day. Trim
12 pretty mushrooms of a uniform size, saving stems for other dishes.
Rinse in cold water very quickly (soaking will drain their natural
juices). Just before serving, ice oysters in the freezer for 4–5 minutes.
Pop an oyster in each mushroom cap, top with sauce, and serve on hot
toast points or lettuce leaves. Or on an hors d'oeuvre tray with plenty
of napkins.

SERVES 2

(Although some greedy gourmands I know would eat all 12 of anything involving oysters!)

TENDER SCALLOPS *AU NATUREL*

Raw scallops taste exactly like cooked scallops, only even more tender. They are delicious.

> *1 cup soy sauce*
> *24 scallops, medium (about 1")*
> *2 tomatoes, sliced*
> *parsley sprigs for garnish*

Put a small dish of soy sauce for dipping with each plate. Serve scallops on chilled plates with parsley and sliced tomatoes. Pass hot bread, or bowls of hot boiled rice.

SERVES 4

SEA SPECIALTIES

CAVIAR SUPPER FOR TWO

Supper by candlelight doesn't have to be elaborate to be romantic.

> *2 ounces cream cheese*   *coarsely ground black pepper*
> *¾ cup sour cream*   *salt to taste*
> *3-ounce jar of red salmon caviar*   *1 avocado, cut in half*
> *1–2 tablespoons grated onion*

Mash the cream cheese, softened to room temperature, with the sour cream. Stir in half of the salmon caviar, the grated onion, a generous amount of pepper, and then taste before adding salt. Spoon into avocado halves. Top with remaining caviar. Serve chilled, with imported crackers, whole-grain crackers, rye "tak," or melba toast rounds. And an interesting cheese. Plus mugs of clam broth.

SERVES 2

Note: This makes a lavish first course at a dinner party.

SEA URCHINS, FRENCH STYLE

Sea-urchin roe is a delicacy prized by many past belief. I first saw it eaten at four A.M. in a restaurant in Les Halles, the former outdoor wholesale produce market of Paris. It was served there in the shells, on a big bed of parsley and greens, and was being consumed with extravagant cries of joy and a lot of French superlatives. Some was offered to me, but I clung to my prejudices and my onion soup, and have always regretted it. It is now considered by many as ranking with the best caviar, and is plentiful in certain coastal regions.

6–8 sea urchins per person (cracked open in shells)
lots of lemon wedges
parsley

a chilled platter lined with greens
shaved ice for platter (optional)

Cover platter with shaved ice and then with chilled greens. Place sea urchins in center and surround with lemon wedges and parsley.

EDMUND GILBERT'S SEA URCHINS

"When skin-diving in Florida, I used to dive down and pick up sea urchins. Later (wearing a glove) I would crack them open, scoop out the orangeish egg masses, squeeze on a lemon brought along for the purpose and pop them into my mouth. Very nourishing and tasty."

6. SALAD ENTREES AND CHEESE DISHES

SALADE NIÇOISE

This renowned dinner or luncheon salad originated in Nice, where the olive groves of the French Riviera, the fresh string beans and potatoes of French gardens, and the tuna of the Mediterranean come together naturally in a country French manner, with fresh-from-the-garden greens. Now it's made in infinite versions and variations all over Europe and the United States, and is excellent winter and summer.

1 small head romaine, Boston, or Bibb lettuce
3–5 small cooked potatoes, peeled and halved
2 7-ounce cans white tuna fish
2 or 3 tomatoes, quartered
¼ pound string beans, halved, cooked lightly, chilled (canned may be used, or raw if very young and tender)

1 green pepper, cut in half rings
½ large red onion, cut in thin rings
12–20 black olives, pitted or not
3 hard-boiled eggs, quartered lengthwise
12 anchovy fillets, drained
capers (optional)
1 cup or less vinaigrette dressing (see Index)

This salad is always tossed at the table, because it is so strikingly hand-some. Arrange it in one big salad bowl. The base is the lettuce, torn into large bite-size leaves. On top of the lettuce, fanning out in pie-slice-like patterns, put the potatoes, tuna (perhaps two sections of this in different places), tomatoes, string beans, green pepper, onion, and black olives. Decorate in the middle and around the edge with the eggs, some tomato, and anchovies. Sprinkle on capers. Beige tuna, brilliant red tomatoes, creamy white potatoes, slashes of green for string beans, shimmering black olives—it's a stunning assortment. Pass dress-ing at the table to pour on individual salads, bring whole salad to table, and pour on dressing and toss there. Warmed French bread and chilled white wine are all that's needed with it for a main course.

SERVES 6–8

LAZY IN-A-HURRY SALADE NIÇOISE

Once having mastered the niceties of salade niçoise, I discovered that I could cheat and make an instant salade niçoise with some of the in-gredients missing and still find it a delightful dinner. All you need is . . .

> *the canned tunafish*
> *the potatoes (canned, if you like)*
> *the black olives*
> *some greens*

. . . and whatever else you happen to have on hand from the formal niçoise recipe.

BETTY PARKER'S
CLASSIC VEGETARIAN GOURMET SALAD

This is dinner. When, like Betty Parker, you've been part of a vege-tarian family for three generations and have a gourmet's love of good food, you gradually evolve a basic salad like this one. This salad has a philosophy, a blend of *subtle* flavors and textures. While you can add and improvise as you like, avoid anything with sharp flavors (like cheddar cheese or pickled anything). The proportions are ½ greens to ½ fillings. All must be icy cold; bowls, dressing, ingredients, even forks.

at least 3 lettuces: ⅓ bunch romaine, ⅓ head redleaf lettuce, ⅓–½ head butter lettuce
1 small zucchini, sliced very thin
6–8 mushrooms, sliced thin
1 or 2 tomatoes, sliced
½ cucumber, sliced thin
¼ green pepper, sliced thin
½ large avocado, sliced
½ cup garbanzo beans
¼–½ cup jicama cut into small cubes
¼–½ cup sunflower seeds, raw and salted

¼ cup sesame seeds, raw or toasted
⅛–¼ cup wheat germ
1 grated hard-cooked egg
½–¾ cup shredded Monterey Jack or mild Tillamook cheese
1 handful alfalfa sprouts
1 handful bean sprouts
croutons (optional)
soy nuts (optional)
No onions!

BASIL DRESSING
⅔ cup mild-flavored oil
⅓ cup vinegar
2 tablespoons water
fresh herbs to taste (or salad seasoning mix)

good pinch basil
¼ teaspoon garlic powder, or 1 clove minced garlic

Make dressing and chill. Put chilled, dried, torn leaves in bottom of salad bowl; arrange other salad ingredients on top. Toss at table.

SERVES 4

FARMER'S CRUNCHY CHOP SUEY SALAD

This old-fashioned salad dates back to the days of the kitchen gardens of Europe and later early America. It's very chunky and crunchy. Traditionally, you picked what was available in your garden that very summer eve, so long as it was crunchy. Everything is chopped, but very coarsely. It's one of those simple suppers everyone can enjoy with today's choice array of very fresh vegetables.

Salt and pepper to taste
5 cups of assorted vegetables, all chopped coarsely, or diced. Use at least 4 of the following: celery, carrots, green pepper, cucumber, mushrooms, onion, zucchini, radishes, maybe a tomato
8 ounces sour cream

Salt and pepper the chopped vegetables, then tumble them in the sour cream, coating all well. Serve on fat lettuce leaves, or in bowls. Add a hearty bread and you've got a hearty supper.

SERVES 4–6

WATERCRESS, HAM, AND CASHEW SALAD

3 bunches (4 cups) watercress, washed, dried, and chilled
½ cup cashews
6 ounces cured (or boiled) ham, cut into strips

8–10 mushrooms, sliced
½ can O & C fried onions
oil-and-vinegar dressing

Chill first 4 ingredients. Before serving, heat onions in oven, and keep hot. Toss chilled ingredients in salad bowl, add dressing, and toss more. Serve with the crushed hot onions scattered on top of each helping. Good with biscuits or Parmesan-buttered bread toasted under the broiler.

SERVES 2–4

SMITHFIELD HAM AND CHEESE SPINACH SALAD WITH MUSTARD DRESSING

6 ounces Smithfield or other cured
  ham, cut into slivers
6 ounces Swiss cheese, cut into
  slivers
½ red onion, sliced
1 tomato, medium, peeled and
  diced

1 big bunch spinach, washed,
  dried, crisped, and torn
3–6 marinated bottled artichoke
  hearts, cut up
1 hard-cooked egg, diced
mustard dressing (see Index)
½ cup croutons

Chill all ingredients. Toss just before serving with dressing and croutons.

SERVES 4

MIXED CABBAGE AND PEANUTS AND CHEESE SALAD

Take the cabbage plunge in a big way—buy one of each: white cabbage, red, savoy, and Chinese. Then make this hearty salad:

¼ head white cabbage
¼ head red cabbage
¼ bunch Chinese cabbage
¼ bunch savoy cabbage
1 hard-cooked egg, minced
½ or more thinly sliced onion
½ pound shredded cheddar
  cheese

1 cup peanuts
1 big handful hot garlicky buttered
  croutons
¾–1 cup vinaigrette dressing (see
  Index), or mayonnaise thinned
  with a little cream.

Wash cabbages. Cut off bottoms of savoy and Chinese cabbage and separate leaves enough to rinse away any dirt. Dry. Shred all very finely just before making salad, add next 5 ingredients, and toss in dressing. This salad, with dressing, can be chilled for quite a while or served at once. It's not as good kept overnight.

SERVES 4–6

SALAMI, GARBANZO, AND SPINACH SALAD

Here's an interesting variation on the classic Italian garbanzo salads. If you make big portions, and use the more generous helping of salami, then it's a refreshing dinner salad. Serve it with instant cream of tomato bisque (see Index), and a garlic or herb bread.

*1 cup or more canned garbanzo
     beans, drained
1 bunch spinach
1 head romaine
1 head butter lettuce*

*¼–½ pound Italian salami
a few slivers Swiss cheese
     (optional)
1 tablespoon sunflower seeds*

DRESSING

*½ teaspon dry mustard,
     moistened
salt to taste
1 garlic clove, minced or crushed*

*2 tablespoons wine vinegar
⅓–½ cup olive oil mixed with
     salad oil*

Mix the dressing and marinate garbanzo beans in it for at least 20 minutes. Drain and reserve dressing. Wash, dry, and tear into pieces spinach, romaine, and butter lettuce. You should have 6 cups or thereabouts. Pile into salad bowl, add beans, and keep in refrigerator till chilled with kitchen towel covering (top towel with a couple of ice cubes). Just before serving, cut salami into sticks and pop under low broiler for a few minutes. At serving time, toss salad with poured-over dressing, then top with sizzly-hot salami, sunflower seeds, and cheese strips and toss that. You might want to pass a little grated Parmesan, but that is optional.

SERVES 4–6

KATHRYN'S SWEET-AND-SPICY
CURRIED FRUIT SALAD

Fruit salad was never so exciting before: a mélange of creamy, spicy-sweet flavors, all in a mood of far, Far Eastern curry. A cool sensation for the palate on a hot summer night. Or at any luncheon feast.

3 apples	*1 orange*
1 pear	*2 bananas*
lemon juice	*¼ cup grated sweetened coconut*
¼ pineapple	*¼ cup cashew pieces*

DRESSING

½ cup mayonnaise	*1 teaspoon or more curry powder*
½ cup sour cream	*¼ teaspoon dry mustard*
2 teaspoons or more honey	

Peel apples and pear and cut into small pieces. Tumble in bowl with a little lemon juice to prevent browning. Top with cut-up pineapple and sliced and peeled orange. Chill. Just before serving, cut up bananas and mix in with other fruit. Combine dressing ingredients and top each serving with dressing. The coconut and cashews are passed at the table.

SERVES 6

Complete this meal with Gourmandaise cheese (or any creamy soft cheese) served with little rolls or wafers.

THE CHEESE PLATTER: AN EFFORTLESS DINNER

Reminiscent of the cold Sunday suppers of an earlier era in America and the relaxed cheese *plattes* of Germany, these effortless cheese plates are perfect for the good and busy life of today. They are basically improvisational, and a translation of the simple but nutritious meat potato-vegetable dining philosophy to a fresh, cold version which uses cheese, seeds, and nuts to replace meat and a fruit and green to replace the vegetable.

A SOFT AND SAVORY CHEESE PLATTE

In Munster, Germany, the local cheese is soft and runny and rich. It is classically served as a *platte* with fresh-chopped onions, a heavy topping of caraway seeds, good honest bread, and a stein of beer—a deliciously satisfying combination that American cheese enthusiasts should not forgo. On each plate goes:

4 ounces super-soft cheese (Brie, Camembert, Liedekranz), softened further at room temperature
2 tablespoons chopped onion
caraway seeds

2 poppy-seed rolls
½ pear and ½ apple (or chunk of pomegranate)
pepper rings, sliced tomato and cucumber

THE RICOTTA CHEESE ITALIAN PLATTER

On each plate goes:

4–6 ounces ricotta-cheese slices
½ jar bottled marinated artichoke hearts
a topping on cheese of 3 slices chopped salami, 1 tablespoon grated provolone cheese, 1 tablespoon chopped fennel (optional)

3 tablespoons garbanzo beans dressed in oil, vinegar, and salt, spooned into 1 tomato, cut open flower-style
4 scallions
finger-cut slices of cantaloupe

THE ENGLISH CHEDDAR PLATE

3 ounces Stilton, Port Salut, and cheddar cheese, sliced thin
a cold boiled potato, parslied
sliced raw baby Brussels sprouts, topped with mayonnaise

sliced onion
sliced tomatoes, topped with sliced raw mushrooms
Waverly wafers (or similar crackers)

THE FRENCH COUNTRY-PICNIC PLATTER

Immortalized in a hundred lush movie scenes and in a thousand paint-
ings, the basic French picnic is an everyday meal that usually features
cheese, a hunk of good bread, fruit, and wine, and always enraptures
the tourist in France. Why not import it? Don't wait for a picnic. Do
as the French do and make this an easy, everyday meal.

On each plate:

*3–6-ounce hunk of good honest
    cheese, an American
    favorite like Tillamook
    or Monterey Jack
a really great bread, from the
    bakery or homemade,
    such as stone-ground
    wheat, a special nut bread,
    or fresh-baked French
    bread*

*1 gorgeous apple, or a basket of
    strawberries, or a bunch of
    grapes
a glass of white wine*

Added to this might be a very simple tossed green salad. Or perhaps a
few sliced raw vegetables on which you pour a little wine and oil, then
sprinkle salt and pepper. Polish it off with, what else? French pastry.

THE RETURN OF THE PEASANT REPAST

An old-fashioned lunch that has picked up a lot of trendy chic lately.
It's a lot of flash with very little fuss.

a bowl of soup
a sliced apple
a few slices of orange and white cheese—perhaps cheddar and Swiss,
    or longhorn, or whatever is handy or a good buy
a glass of red wine, probably a Burgundy or something with a touch of
    heartiness

CHEESE FONDUE
A VEGETARIAN FEAST

an assortment of 5 or 6 of the following, cut in bite-size chunks: peeled cucumber, zucchini, cauliflowerets, broccoli flowerets, asparagus tips, cherry tomatoes, celery, small whole mushrooms, jerusalem artichokes

unsliced French bread
½ cup milk (¾ cup if wine not used)
¼ cup white wine (optional)
½ teaspoon Worcestershire sauce
¼ teaspoon dry mustard
dash white pepper
1 cup mayonnaise
2 cups shredded cheddar cheese

Wash and chill vegetables and cut into chunks. Cut bread into chunks. Melt the cheese-fondue ingredients in a double boiler over low heat, stirring occasionally, until cheese is melted and mixture is hot.

Serve fondue in the pot on a trivet at the table, or serve in a fondue pot. Give everyone a long fondue fork for dipping. Pass a bowl of poppy seeds or sesame seeds to sprinkle on some cheesy bits.

SERVES 4

NUTS AND SEEDS—THINK OF THEM AS DINNER

All nuts are delicious eaten raw as well as roasted. They are loaded with flavor, as well as protein and many other nutrients, and taste so good (and are eaten in candy and in desserts so often) that we forget how valuable they are as a main dish. If you serve them with a little rice, beans, bread, milk, or cheese, the protein ranks with filet mignon nutritionally.

Children adore nuts. If they seem an extravagance for children's snacking, consider their nutritive virtues and remember that some of the junk foods children snack on have little or no food value. Nuts are worth the money.

All of the following nuts and seeds can be eaten raw. For some snacking suggestions, see pages 53, 55.

acorns	*lychee nuts*
almonds	*macadamia nuts*
beechnuts	*peanuts*
Brazil nuts	*pecans*
butternuts	*pine nuts*
cashews	*pistachio nuts*
chestnuts	*pumpkin seeds*
chia seeds	*sesame seeds*
coconuts	*sunflower seeds*
filberts	*walnuts, black*
hickory nuts	*walnuts, English*

STORAGE OF NUTS

In the shell, nuts keep well from 4 to 7 months. Shelled nuts can be kept in the refrigerator for 1 year, in the freezer for 2 years. This makes it most economical to purchase nuts in quantity at lower prices.

NUT ROLL À LA 1920

This far-out nut roll dates from California in the 1920s. If you can't find pignolias, substitute other rich, chewy nuts like cashews, macadamias, pecans, etc. This dish makes sense for the busy days of today, since it waits obligingly in the refrigerator. It's reasonably light and not sweet, so you can follow it with a rich fruit dessert.

3/4 cup minced celery (strings removed)
6 ounces pignolias, crushed
1/4 cup mashed avocado
2 tablespoons chopped green onion
2 tablespoons finely minced parsley

2 tablespoons mayonnaise
garlic powder
a pinch of sage
salt, if at all, to taste

Shape, after mixing well, into roll, and wrap in mayonnaise-greased sheet of wax paper or aluminum foil. Refrigerate at least 2 hours, or all day, so that flavors can blend. To serve, slice on a platter lined with salad greens. Garnish with grated cheese, grated lemon, black olives, or tomato wedges—anything fresh that's handy. Serve with big crackers or old-fashioned saltines, or whole-grain bread cut into big cubes and toasted under the broiler.

SERVES 2

JOAN BURNS
SWEET AND NUTTY SALAD WITH
POPPY-SEED DRESSING

This delectable creation tastes as good as a dessert, but it's an all-in-one party dinner. You may never notice, but it's drenched with protein.

6 handfuls salad greens
4 ounces shelled pecans
6–8 ounces shelled walnuts
4 shredded carrots
6 ounces Jack cheese, cut in sticks

1 cup tightly packed alfalfa sprouts
raisins
candied papaya or candied dates,
*   chopped*
1 avocado, sliced just before serving

POPPY-SEED DRESSING

1¼ cup sugar
2 teaspoons dry mustard
2 teaspoons salt
⅔ cup vinegar

3 tablespoons onion juice (or grated onion)
2 cups vegetable oil
¼ cup poppy seeds

Arrange a mélange of the salad ingredients on 6 plates, starting with greens at base. Put all dressing ingredients except oil and poppy seeds in blender at low speed and gradually add the oil as for making mayonnaise (a few drops at a time). Gradually blend in poppy seeds. Pour dressing generously over each plate and serve with a good hearty bread or toasted cheese wafers.

SERVES 6

7. VEGETABLES AND GREENERY

VEGETABLES IN THE RAW

Who has not blanked out a hundred times over what vegetable to serve at dinner tonight? Too often, everyone's repertoire is limited by tastes, prejudices, and simple boredom through repetition. Once you open your mind to their mind-boggling diversity and deliciousness, raw vegetables are an inspired solution for at least half the days of the year. Mildly liked vegetables often take on ravishingly delicious new personalities as raw vegetables, as many a low-calorie-seeker has joyfully discovered.

The crispy freshness of raw vegetables plays beautifully against the soft richness of cooked dishes. And they're easy to prepare.

And the nutrition dividends are formidable. Vegetables are all bursting with vitamins and minerals, the nutrients that are most vulnerable to the ravages of cooking.

Traditionally we think of raw vegetables as a snack or appetizer. But why stop there? Why spend time fussing in the kitchen to cook a dinner vegetable that can be eaten with astonishing simplicity and goodness raw?

Remember that raw vegetables of all kinds are in their element in all salads. And the best picnics should always include a lavish array of raw foods, a thrifty as well as delicious idea, because, unlike soggy sandwiches and travel-weary cold chicken, raw vegetables, if not consumed on the picnic spot, come home to see another day as a cooked vegetable.

Slice raw vegetable servings onto dinner plates instead of cooked vegetables. And finally, expand the horizons of your raw vegetable tray, with its tempting side dips. (See Index.)

ASPARAGUS IN THE RAW

Just at the end of midwinter, when you're bored with the same winter vegetables, along comes one of the most unusual and exciting: asparagus. Asparagus is elegant at any price, but do watch for the height of the season, when the supply is plentiful and the prices mouthwateringly low. Then, for a few short weeks, you can debauch yourself and go on asparagus binges.

Use only fresh asparagus in raw-food recipes. Both thin and medium stalks are good raw. To be sure they're good and fresh, ask the produce man.

Wash the stalks well and break them off at the base where they snap off naturally (if stalks are not crisp, asparagus is not fresh enough). Wash well, discarding stalk ends (or save for soup).

Serve chilled on raw-vegetable platter, or pass as an appetizer. Drizzled with dressing, they make a refreshingly new dinner salad. Wrap them in thin slices of ham if you like. *Marvelous with all dips!*

VIRGINIA'S
ASPARAGUS WITH ROQUEFORT SOUR CREAM

40 *medium or thin stalks asparagus*　　*salt or seasoned salt to taste*
　　(2–2½ *pounds*)　　　　　　　*white pepper* (*optional*)
2 *ounces Roquefort cheese*　　　　*sprinkling of cayenne pepper*
8-*ounce container sour cream*

Wash asparagus and snap off stalks, then trim. Bring a pot of water to a rolling boil, plunge in the asparagus, and let boil for *exactly* 60 seconds. Pour off water and *immediately* plunge asparagus into ice water (with ice cubes) to arrest cooking and keep tender-crisp texture. Chill until cold. Prepare dip by mashing Roquefort cheese into a little bit of sour cream, adding more sour cream and salting to taste as you go along. This makes a striking hors d'oeuvre or first course. At the dinner table, serve on individual plates with Roquefort spooned over as a sauce.

SERVES 6

LIANG-PAN-LU-SUN
CHINESE ASPARAGUS SALAD

*1½ pounds young fresh asparagus, each stalk no more than ½" in
     diameter*
4 teaspoons soy sauce
1 teaspoon sugar
2 teaspoons sesame oil

Wash asparagus and snap off stalk bottoms. Discard ends. Slice remaining stalks in 1½″ lengths, using roll-cut method: Place stalk on wooden board and make first diagonal cut. Now "roll" asparagus ¼ of way around (a quarter turn) and make next diagonal slice. Roll another quarter turn and slice diagonally again. This is very important in all Oriental cuisine, since it exposes the interior of the food evenly to the blanching heat in the most efficient way. You should end up with about 3 cups of asparagus.

Bring a pot of water to a rolling boil and drop the asparagus into the boiling water for *1 minute*. Lift out and plunge immediately into ice water. Spread asparagus on a towel, and pat dry. In a more-than-3-cup-size bowl, combine the soy sauce, sugar, and sesame oil, and mix until the sugar is completely dissolved. Add the asparagus and toss thoroughly in dressing. Chill, tumbling asparagus in dressing every so often, for 2–3 hours. Garnish each serving with a fresh chrysanthemum.

SERVES 4–6, OR 6–8 AS PART OF BUFFET

AVOCADOS

What can be served at seven different courses, goes well with at least a thousand foods, tastes smooth or sweet or creamy or spicy, is ostentatiously rich in nutrients and flavor—but quite modest in calories? The avocado, of course. It has become one of the most elegant convenience foods around, for the obliging avocado, although warmed in an occasional recipe, is never cooked. It is *perfect* raw, just as nature created it. And a delectable soulmate of practically every food you can think of. No wonder avocados are the pampered darlings of lavish banquets, barefoot picnics and salad bowls.

A ready-to-eat avocado is one that is firm but not hard, and yields slightly to your hand's pressure. A soft-firm avocado is also ready to eat. A very soft avocado is okay for guacamole. Hard avocados will soften nicely at home at room temperature or in a dark bag. Once ripened, avocados belong in the refrigerator, where they will keep for several days.

NOTE ON PREPARING AVOCADOS

Avocados peel and slice easily, but should be brushed with lemon or lime juice if they are to be held for more than half an hour, or they will darken (like apples). Mashed avocado mixtures, like guacamoles, will retain their soft green color if you immerse the avocado pit in the mixture until serving time.

TWO PRETTY SLICES OF AVOCADO LIFE

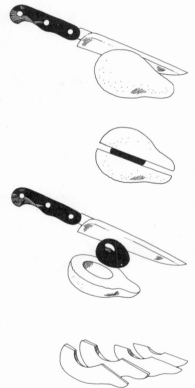

1. Cut lengthwise around the avocado, pressing through to the pit. Cup your hands around each half and gently twist to separate halves.

2. Snap knife into pit. Twist and it will lift out easily.

3. Peel by holding half flat on palm of one hand, while you slit and peel skin in strips from half.

4. Slice lengthwise, still holding half in palm of your hand, or set on wooden board or plate. Or cut into dice.

OR

Proceed as in steps 1 and 2, above, but do not peel for many half-shell avocado dishes. Simply spoon out the avocado from the shell, which is very easy to do.

AVOCADOS WITH LIME WEDGES

A beautiful avocado, like a beautiful woman, needs little dressing. Often forgotten in favor of more dazzling recipes, this classic way of eating avocados is delicious and easy.

1 avocado
1 lime, quartered

Just before serving, slice avocado in half and remove pit. Squeeze on lime juice, and spoon out of shell. Some add a little salt.

SERVES 2

AVOCADOS VINAIGRETTE

Another avocado classic, and deservedly so. There are few more satisfying taste sensations than a bite of avocado with a glazing of good vinaigrette dressing. It's a sublime match.

2 avocados, slightly soft
¾ cup vinaigrette dressing (see Index) or your own favorite oil- and vinegar-dressing
a few capers or bits of bacon for garnish (optional)

Peel your avocado very gently and carefully. Cut in half, again carefully. Knife seed and remove by twisting free. Place avocado half face down on plate, and gently slice in clean arcs from top to bottom, fanning out slices. Do each avocado in this way, then drizzle dressing so all slices are covered. The slices should fall in a symmetrical array on dish. This is the key to its beauty. Garnish.

SERVES 4

AVOCADO SWIMMING POOLS

2 avocados, halved and unpeeled, pit removed
oil-and-vinegar dressing (or your favorite dressing)

Fill the avocado halves until they're swimming in spicy dressing. Then take spoon and take a dip.

SERVES 4

Men enjoy preparing and eating avocados like this. It is really just the 2-second version of avocados vinaigrette, often made with whatever dressing happens to be around.

AVOCADO AND GRAPEFRUIT WITH ORANGE SAUCE

4 ounces cream cheese
2 ounces orange juice concen-
*   trate, thawed (or more to*
*   taste)*
2 avocados

2 grapefruit, peeled and sectioned
*   (or very good canned*
*   grapefruit sections)*
salt to taste
4 large lettuce leaves

Blend softened cream cheese with orange juice concentrate until it has a tangy, creamy bland flavor. Moisten with a little milk if it's too thick. Peel and slice avocado and grapefruit just before serving. On four plates, arrange avocado and grapefruit on lettuce and pour on orange sauce.

SERVES 4

AVOCADO, THE UNEXPECTED GREEN VEGETABLE
A pretty addition to any dinner plate: Just slice it and add a wedge of lime. Or put avocado slices on baked potatoes, spaghetti, or whatever occurs to you.

BEETS

TOSSED SHREDDED BEET SALAD

Try this instead of the usual green salad with broiled beef or simmered meat dishes.

½ cup sour cream
2 tablespoons milk
1–2 teaspoons prepared horse-
    radish
¼ teaspoon salt
dash of pepper

6 coarsely shredded or grated
    small raw beets (about 3
    cups)
1 shredded or grated tart apple
sliced blanched almonds, walnuts,
    or sunflower seeds
chopped parsley

Combine and blend sour cream, milk, horseradish, salt, and pepper; set aside. Mix beets with apple. Add dressing and toss, then chill. This salad can be chilled for a few hours or just a few minutes. Just before serving, sprinkle with nuts or seeds. Top with parsley.

SERVES 4–6

BROCCOLI IN THE RAW

This brilliant green plant is actually *two* vegetables: lavish-looking flowerets and sleek green stalks. Broccoli is simply great with all manner of dips and dunks—and quite good all by itself or with a tiny squeeze of lemon. Knowing that broccoli is bursting with good nutrition and low in calories, you can gorge yourself on it with ease. It's also rich in Vitamin A and good for your complexion. It keeps nicely for a few days, not being one of the very fragile vegetables, and the price is right since broccoli is easy to grow, ships well, and has a long low-priced season in most areas.

Look for brilliantly deep-green flowerets. If they're starting to lighten or turn yellowish, pass them by.

PREPARING BROCCOLI

Trim ends of stalks, perhaps while still in wire bunch-wrap if your market packs them that way. In one cut, slice flowerets away from stalks, usually leaving about ½″–1″ stalks on the flowerets. Swish all in sink filled with cold water for just a few seconds. Shake, bag, and refrigerate, refrigerate the stalks separately.

BROCCOLI FLOWERETS

These broccoli flowers (my children call them "trees") are delicious finger food just as is. You might sprinkle on a little salt or seasoned salt, or a squeeze of lemon.

BROCCOLI FLOWERETS VINAIGRETTE WITH EGG

This is a French dish with an Oriental touch, in which you blanch the raw broccoli in the Chinese manner. It will make the greens more brilliant, and lend just a hint of tender-crispy texture.

1 pound broccoli flowerets   *½ clove crushed garlic*
½ cup oil   *salt and pepper to taste*
2–3 tablespoons wine vinegar   *2 or 3 hard-cooked eggs*
½ teaspoon dry mustard

Plunge broccoli into lots of the rapidly boiling water, and count off 60 seconds. Quickly remove and plunge into icy water. Remove from icy water immediately, drain, and chill (it will be almost cold already).

Mix an oil-and-vinegar dressing, adding spices. Stir in chopped hard-cooked egg. Toss broccoli in dressing and chill for an hour or more. Place on individual plates. Drizzle dressing on top, being sure to have some bits of egg showing against the green of the broccoli.

SERVES 4–6

For guests, or for fun, garnish with tomato half slices, radish roses, and notched cucumber slices.

BROCCOLI FLOWERETS WITH GREEN MAYONNAISE

Blend some mayonnaise in blender or by hand with 2 or 3 tablespoons of chopped parsley, chives, broccoli flowerets (use one of the ones you're serving). Use your own homemade mayonnaise or bottled mayonnaise. Or use greenery mayonnaise (see Index).

BROCCOLI FLOWERETS WITH DIPS

There couldn't be a prettier addition to any raw vegetable platter, and broccoli goes with all dips.

BROCCOLI STALKS

A little-known but delectable addition to your raw-vegetable platter, broccoli stalks are one of those raw-vegetable surprises you should keep to yourself, divulging their identity only when everyone comments on how tender-crisp and good they taste. My cousin, Fran Hansford, takes a fiendish pleasure in serving them to people who hate broccoli.

Peel the stalks first. The peel is fairly thick, and you will find it pulls away quite cleanly when you lift it with a knife. Cut peeled stalks in half if they are long, then sliver into dipping sticks about ¼" thick. Serve them as you would celery, with literally every dip, or simply with salt.

BRUSSELS SPROUTS IN THE RAW

Brussels sprouts are terribly English, and terrible when they're overcooked. Norman Rossington, a marvelous English actor, confessed that even the English often enjoy them more raw.

Members of the cabbage family, Brussels sprouts are really just like tiny, doll-size cabbages. You should shop for them like cabbages, looking for tight little heads and a minimum of tired outer leaves. Their season is short, so pounce on them when you see them. All they need is a good sloshing about in cold water and they're ready to eat. And surprisingly good!

Two more thoughts about Brussels sprouts: They're simply loaded with Vitamin C, especially when raw (some Vitamin C is lost in heat-ing). And when the green leaves of summer salads fade away, Brussels sprouts are just starting to arrive on the market . . .

BRUSSELS SPROUTS VINAIGRETTE
Quarter them, chill, and toss in a pristine vinaigrette dressing with a pinch of sugar and minced hard-cooked egg. Sprinkle Parmesan cheese or chopped peanuts on top if you like. Allow 5 or 6 sprouts and half a hard-cooked egg per person.

BRUSSELS SPROUTS COLESLAW WITH GRATED CHEESE
Any coleslaw (or "cold slaw") recipe will also work crisply with Brussels sprouts instead of cabbage. For that matter, so will any salad calling for cabbage. Try topping with grated cheese.

BRUSSELS SPROUTS WITH CHESTNUTS OR WALNUTS
These nuts have an affinity for Brussels sprouts. Slice sprouts thinly and toss with nuts in a spicy oil-and-vinegar or a sour-cream dressing.

CABBAGE

Cabbages are just one member of a dynasty of crisp and aggressive vegetables called *Brassica* that have reigned supreme in any number of cuisines since before the early Greco-Roman civilizations.

Cabbage is the matriarch of this genus, but so far as eating in the raw is concerned, the recipes used for cabbages should also be used for the other members of the genus, including savoy cabbage, Chinese cabbage, Brussels sprouts, and red cabbage. All are powerhouses of nutrition, tending toward lusty rather than delicate personalities. Enjoy them all in the raw.

An interesting note: These members of the *Brassica* genus are often referred to as "strong-flavored" vegetables, partially because they have a strong odor when overcooked (because of the release of sulfur compounds). Raw, they're bright in flavor, crunchy in texture. The cabbage is a dramatic example of how totally different the cooked and raw flavors of a vegetable can be.

CABBAGE: THE INSTANT DINNER VEGETABLE AND SNACK

When the Walrus in *Alice's Adventures in Wonderland* spoke of "cabbages and kings" he had the right idea, for it is a royal vegetable in the raw.

Icy wedges, cut away from the core, make a refreshing snack at any time of the day, and an instant dinner vegetable. A nice idea is to put a half head of cabbage on a cutting plate, with a sharp small knife, in the refrigerator right at eye level. Cover with plastic wrap or a glass dome. Then whoever drifts by with hunger pangs has something refreshing right there to be sliced in a second.

Think of *all* the cabbages as super-beauty snacks. Cabbage has a very exclusive group of trace nutrients that are beneficial to pretty skin. The Russians dine (and, indeed, breakfast and lunch!) every day on something cabbagy, and they are noted for blooming complexions (it's not just all that cold that brings out the roses in their cheeks).

Children enjoy plain sliced cabbage as finger food. They can even be permitted to carry it about the house, since it is not messy.

RED CABBAGE, RED ONION, AND TOMATO SALAD

1½ cups red cabbage, shredded   ¼ cup oil-and-vinegar dressing
¼ cup red onion, thinly sliced   ¼ teaspoon brown sugar (optional)
1 small tomato, chopped

Toss all together and marinate in refrigerator for 3 hours or so. Great with a meat entree.

SERVES 2–4

AMAZING 60-SECOND COLE SLAW
THE FASTEST SLAW IN THE WEST

Among the ten thousand variations of cole slaw, some very fancy, we forget the simple sturdy wonder that made cole slaw a national institution to begin with: It's cheap and good and *quick,* and it won't wilt if you save some for tomorrow.

But *quick* is the trick that turns on cole-slaw makers everywhere.

Whip out the cabbage (half a small head) and slice thinly. (Thirty seconds.) Whip out the mayonnaise, moisten with a dab of milk or cream, and toss. (Thirty seconds.) That's all.

VERY-CHOPPED COLE SLAW WITH CHOPPED PEANUTS

½ head cabbage
1 handful peanuts
¼ cup mayonnaise moistened with milk or cream
salt and pepper
squeeze of lemon

Core cabbage half and place cabbage flat side down on a cutting board and slice very, very thin. Then slice crosswise, too. Chop peanuts with heavy knife on cutting board, or in blender. Mix gently with mayonnaise moistened by milk (this is often not necessary if you're using your own homemade mayonnaise). Add salt and pepper and lemon to taste. Sometimes a pinch of brown sugar is good with this. Chill before serving.

SERVES 4–6

CARROTS

Carrots are a familiar cliché on all vegetable trays, but don't take them for granted. Carrots deserve their universal popularity for a number of reasons. They keep beautifully, and taste wonderfully sweet—naturally, since they are one of the richest natural-sugar foods you can eat. When babies turn into toddlers who know how to open refrigerator doors, try putting a dish of raw carrot sticks within their reach. They'll eat them like candy. And when you get the late-movie sugar blues, keep a bowl of carrot curls or carrot-raisin grated salad handy in the refrigerator for a marvelous snack that doesn't leave crumbs in bed.

Carrots are not only good for your sweet tooth, they're just plain good for your teeth, period. Eating crunchy raw carrots is like brushing your teeth.

Will they curl your hair, as some mothers promise? Probably not. But every 3½ ounces delivers a staggering 11,000 units of Vitamin A, so they will surely brighten your eyes and pamper your skin.

SHOPPING NOTE

Freshly picked, carrots are super-sweet. As time goes by, the natural sugar turns into starch and that sweet taste fades. For eating raw, look for young, crisp-hard, tops-on carrots.

Try raw fresh carrot juice. Delicious! It's carried by all health-food stores and some supermarkets. If you have a juicer, of course, you can make your own.

CARROTS VINAIGRETTE

Au Petit Café, a revered Los Angeles restaurant, serves this exquisitely good version of carrots vinaigrette.

> *12 carrots*
> *½ cup oil-and-vinegar dressing*
> *minced parsley*
> *1 clove garlic, minced*

Shred carrots very, very fine (gossamer fine). The new kitchen shredders such as Cuisinart do a fabulous job. Marinate shredded carrots for an hour or so in dressing, to which you have added the parsley and garlic. Serve with dressing spooned on top, on a lettuce-leaf bed.

SERVES 4

CAULIFLOWER

Small wonder that one of America's favorite raw vegetables for dipping is cauliflowerets. They are so joyfully crunchy, with a flavor that has a faintly peppery tang, and taste great alone or with any dip.

When you're serving cauliflower raw, look for very white heads. Don't worry about a little trace of dirt on them; just wash well, scraping any spots very lightly with the sharp edge of a knife. Cut out the core and save for mashed cauliflower or soup. (Or cut core into cubes and spear with toothpicks.)

CAULIFLOWERETS DRESSED IN HOT CHEDDAR

An unexpected dinner vegetable, and quite as good as the usual cooked cauliflower with cheese sauce.

6 ounces cheddar cheese, grated   *Worcestershire sauce (optional)*
a little beer (cream cheese may be   *1 head cauliflower, broken into*
*   substituted)*   *flowerets*
a little mustard

Melt the cheddar with beer and mustard until saucy. Taste and add a little Worcestershire sauce if needed. Drizzle on crispy cauliflower on individual dinner plates. Good with any meat dish.

SERVES 4

EARLY SPRING CAULIFLOWER SALAD

1–1½ cups cauliflowerets
¾–1 cup asparagus tips
½ cup garbanzo beans, canned (or croutons)
½ cup shredded cheddar cheese

LEMON DRESSING

1 egg (raw or boiled for 1 minute)
¾ cup soy oil or salad oil
2 tablespoons lemon juice
dash of vinegar

salt and pepper to taste
½ chopped green pepper
10 ripe olives, pitted, sliced in
rings
1 pimiento, finely chopped

Wash cauliflower and cut off flower tops, or break it apart with your fingers and just trim where needed. Cut asparagus into tips 2½"–3" long. Assemble cauliflower, asparagus, beans, and cheese in salad bowl.

Mix dressing, beating egg well into the oil and lemon juice, then stirring in vinegar, salt and pepper, green pepper, olives, and pimiento. Dressing can be tossed into salad and allowed to chill for a while before being served.

SERVES 4–6

CELERIAC (CELERY ROOT)

This is an intriguing vegetable. It comes as a rather large, forbidding root. Once peeled, it reveals itself as a somewhat tenderer cousin of celery: white, crispy, delicate, and quietly elegant. Julienned into thin sticks after peeling, it is a sophisticated member of the raw-vegetable tray.

CELERIAC SPICY STICKS
MARINATED CELERY ROOT

This recipe makes celeriac the showpiece in a tangy mustard dressing.

2 large celery roots
1 cup oil-and-vinegar dressing
1 tablespoon prepared Dijon-type
mustard

2 tablespoons chopped capers
1 tablespoon grated onion
1 tablespoon chopped parsley
1 hard-cooked egg, chopped

Peel celery roots and cut into julienne strips. Mix dressing from remaining ingredients. Immerse in dressing, cover, and marinate for 1 hour out of refrigerator. Serve chilled, as part of hors d'oeuvre tray or with crackers or thin pumpernickel.

SERVES 6

SALADE TOURANGELLE

1 celeriac	*mustard*
1 firm boiled potato per person	*chervil, finely chopped*
1 head curly chicory (white parts)	*parsley, finely chopped*
mayonnaise	

Scrub celeriac with stiff brush and peel. Slice into fine julienne strips. If you are using only a few potatoes, do not use all the celeriac if it is a large one. Slice the potatoes and put in a salad bowl with the celeriac and some of the whitest part of curly chicory. Make a dressing of mayonnaise, adding some mustard moistened in a little water (use this water to thin mayonnaise if needed). Pour dressing on salad, then sprinkle generously with chervil (use dried if you do not have fresh) and parsley. I like to grate on a little onion, too, although that's not the way it's made in France. Pass salad in bowl at table.

SERVES 3–6

CORN ON THE COB, TENDER AND YOUNG

From time immemorial, children have plucked young ears from the cornfield and savored their fresh, natural-sugar sweetness. The corn must be fresh-picked by you, or at least gotten to you within a few hours. Your own garden or roadside vegetable stands in season and certain very select gourmet produce markets are the best sources. Good as is, or with a bit of salt.

CUCUMBERS

Sun-warmed, breeze-cooled, the fresh cucumbers are brought in before dusk from my father's organic garden. Everyone pounces on them and eats them immediately in his own favorite way. For my father, simple mayonnaise, and he quarters the cucumbers lengthwise, having just rinsed them off at the sink. For Veida, yogurt must be mixed with the mayonnaise, or she tries her thousandth just-created dip. Wesley, the purist, slices his crosswise and eats some with salt and pepper only, some with dip. Ten-year-old Adam sneers at the sauces—cucumber should be eaten without anything on it (he may be right!). Thirteen-year-old Graham wants lots of rich guacamole, or lots of blue-cheese dip. You can eat cucumbers for years without really tasting them, especially if you insist on soaking their juices out with salt, pressing them, squeezing them, deluging them with vinegar, and just generally massacring them. That's *after* we throw away half of the cucumber by overpeeling it and scooping out the whole center of tender, deliciously edible seeds! Why don't we just eat them as is?

CUCUMBERS JUNGLE JIM

These go packed into the forest, the wilds, the beach, the back of the car, or simply into the urban jungle, with a knife and a bottle of mayonnaise. Quartered lengthwise, they dip nicely into the jar. Or peel them thinly with a potato peeler, leaving as much of the greenish color as you can (you only want to remove the bare outer green skin).

CUCUMBERS GRAHAM

Cut into dipping sticks and serve with guacamole spiked with a little mayonnaise (see Index). Always make the chunks big enough so you get the full flavor of the cucumber.

ARMENIAN OR EUROPEAN CUCUMBERS

These are sometimes flamboyantly curved, other times straight deep-ridged, rather long, light- to mid-green, and not to be missed by cucumber buffs. The Armenian cucumber, not easily found in many markets, is well worth inquiring for. It is very, *very* crisp and crunchy, not at all bitter, and needs no peeling (the skin is tender). Use it in all your cucumber recipes but do try it plain—sliced, with not even a dash of salt, but a zesty lemon grating on top.

CUCUMBERS WITH SOUR CREAM AND NUTS

1 cucumber
milk (or lemon juice if you like
added tartness)
4 ounces sour cream

grated lemon peel
chopped almonds or walnuts
black or golden raisins (a Middle
Eastern touch)

SERVES 2–4

Chop up the cucumber very fine, adding a little milk to thin the sour cream, and you have cucumber sauce, which is good on grilled meats and fish, nice on cold poached salmon and fish mousse, on tomatoes cut open like flowers, and even just on buttered bread.

ENDIVE, BELGIAN

Belgian means Belgian. This true endive is actually flown from Belgium, where the soil is exactly right for this most elite of salad vegetables. It costs an astonishing amount at our markets and at the most discriminating restaurants, but it is well worth it for special occasions.

It is popular in Europe braised, but here we have decided it is even better served simply and quietly, in a chaste vinaigrette sauce that permits the slightly bitter, unforgettable character of the endive to sparkle against the bland tang of the sauce. There are those who would argue as to whether the endive should be sliced or not. I think it's a crime to slice it, since it has graceful and small leaves that fan out naturally on a plate in the most delicate way. And the curve of each leaf holds the dressing in.

This small, white, cone-shaped, tightly wrapped series of scooplike leaves should not be confused with the American curly endive, which is a very good green that looks more like chicory or romaine than it does like endive from Belgium.

SHOPPING FOR BELGIAN ENDIVE

The white of the Belgian endive should be immaculate, the outer leaves unwilted (you use all the leaves). Just rinse and dry endive when you bring it home, and put in crisper. Do not store in refrigerator very long; after all, it's already come a long way, and time makes inroads on its delicate flavor.

BELGIAN ENDIVE VINAIGRETTE

This should be served with a certain amount of dash and aplomb. Certainly not with an everyday casserole. It is delightful with wine, but too delicate to serve with the lusty character of beer. Serve it as a separate course, all by itself, fanned out on individual plates chilled in the freezer or refrigerator. It would be a suitable touch to chill the salad forks, too.

1 Belgian endive
1 hard-cooked egg, minced
½–¾ cup vinaigrette dressing (see Index)

1 teaspoon extremely finely minced parsley
parsley sprig for garnish (optional)

Break off the endive leaves one by one, trimming any tiny loose ends. Arrange them in fan pattern on chilled plates, with smallest leaves on top if you have no more room on plate. Just before serving, stir minced egg into dressing, and spoon dressing gently over the leaves, being sure to cover as much surface as possible. Sprinkle on the tiny bits of parsley and the garnish, and serve. Candlelight shows off the shimmer of the dressing on the pale-white leaves.

SERVES 2

DIPPED BELGIAN ENDIVE

For a casual repast, arrange the endive leaves on a platter, with a dipping bowl of vinaigrette dressing (see Index) that you have processed in the blender with 2 anchovies. Serve with big paper napkins and have each person dip his endive into dressing, sweeping to bottom of dip bowl to get the flavor of the anchovies. Good with mugs of hot broth spiked with cream sherry, Pernod on the rocks, or Cinzano on the rocks.

FLOWERS IN THE RAW

Flower-nibbling dates back to Roman times, and was popular in Elizabethan days as well. In the days of the kitchen garden, flowers found their way into various recipes. Now flowers are making a colorful comeback in showy salads. Your garden may be blooming with gourmet delights. Sprinkle a few of these on your summer salads:

chrysanthemums	*nasturtium leaves, young and small*
clover	*orchids*
daisies	*pansies*
dandelions	*rose petals*
honeysuckle	*snapdragons*
lemon blossoms	*tulips (take out center)*
marigolds	*violets*
nasturtium flowers and buds	*yucca flowers*

These petals are nutritious, delicious, and beautiful conversation pieces on salads. There are only two rules: 1) Use flowers that were not sprayed with chemicals. 2) Do not guess, or use strange flowers, without checking with your state agricultural service. Some flowers are poisonous; a few are deadly. Those on the list above are some of the flowers traditionally and safely eaten.

FLOWER SALAD IN CHAMPAGNE DRESSING

10 nasturtiums, petals only, and a few tender, small nasturtium leaves (or marigold petals if nasturtiums not available)
4 roses, petals only
a few daisies, petals only, or violets (optional)

¼ head romaine
1 head butter lettuce
½ head redleaf lettuce
10–12 medium mushrooms
¾ cup oil-and-vinegar dressing with 3 tablespoons champagne added

Wash flowers and remove petals. Discard stems and cores. Wash greens, dry them, and tear them into salad bowl. Wash and slice mushrooms. Scatter mushrooms on top of greens in salad bowl, with flowers on top of that. Bring to table. Dress and toss just before serving. Serve with the rest of the champagne!

SERVES 6

Note: Other flowers may be substituted depending on availability. This salad glows with chrysanthemums in the fall and winter, and so on. Use fresh, unsprayed flowers only.

GARLIC IN THE RAW . . . EVERYWHERE

Garlic lovers are quick to justify their passion by informing you that garlic is marvelous for the digestion as well as the palate. They've been claiming this for twenty centuries, so it must be true. If you like garlic, it belongs in many salad dressings, dips, and spreads. Eat a little parsley after garlic dishes, and it will instantly clear your breath.

GINGER ROOT

> Here, sweetheart, here's some green ginger for thee.
> —BEAUMONT AND FLETCHER,
> contemporaries of Shakespeare's

Fresh (green) ginger root, a tropical plant root, is a familiar ingredient in Chinese cuisine, and now its seductive sweet hotness is appearing in many dishes inspired by a love of Oriental flavors. From communes to the chic-est bistros, ginger is in. Look for one at a specialty market. It's gnarled on the outside, and pungently pale green on the inside. To use your fresh ginger root, just grate a bit of it as your mood or the recipe calls for, after carefully washing it first. Peeling isn't necessary.

STORAGE OF FRESH GINGER ROOT

There you are, having sparingly used a mere bit of your ginger root. What to do with the rest of it? A very gingery cousin of mine, Fran Hansford, told me. Just put it in a Baggie and pop it in your freezer! There it will stay, for at least a year. Every time a recipe calls for ginger, you just whip it out of the freezer, grate it, then return the rest to the freezer. And no powder can ever duplicate the pungent, exotic appeal of fresh-grated ginger root in even the simplest dish. Use it in a ginger-soy dip (see Index) or grate it over green or fruit salads.

HORSERADISH IN THE RAW

Horseradish is a root of famed hot and pungent flavor, often purchased as a very good sharp bottled sauce. The flavor of fresh horseradish is quite different—and delicious. Horseradish is meant to be eaten in the raw: in dips, grated into spreads, passed as the most aggressive of hot condiments. A little will make you blissfully happy; a lot will make you cry, literally. True horseradish mavens love it with almost anything short of dessert. For boiled beef, it's a classic. And since its pungent kick clears the sinuses quite efficently, try it on your next cold!

Preferably, buy a small root for the most tender flavor. A larger one is all right, but you must cut out a bit of the woody center core. Wash and clean your horseradish root thoroughly with a stiff wire brush or plastic Tuffy pad, so it will grate a snowy white. Grate on a hand grater. Mixed with a bit of lemon juice (or white vinegar) and sugar, grated horseradish can be kept for several weeks in the refrigerator (tightly sealed) and passed as a condiment or used in making horseradish sauces and spreads. Extra horseradish root keeps in the freezer.

DELICATE HORSERADISH CREAM DIP

½ teaspoon or more grated horseradish
1 cup sour cream
salt and lemon juice to taste

Add horseradish to sour cream. Taste and perhaps add a bit more. The idea is to have a fluffy tang of horseradish in the cream.

DEVASTATING HORSERADISH CREAM DIP WITH CANNIBAL STEAK

a lot of horseradish, grated
a little sour cream
salt and lemon juice (optional)
½ pound very fresh top sirloin, diced and speared with toothpicks

Make dip as in previous recipe and serve with chilled steak cubes and something cool to drink.

HORSERADISH SPREAD ON BLACK BREAD

1 3-ounce package cream cheese, softened   *½ teaspoon grated fresh*
2 tablespoons dairy sour cream   *horseradish*
1 tablespoon snipped parsley or chives   *salt to taste*

Beat together the cream cheese and sour cream. Stir in parsley or chives, horseradish, and salt. Spread on thin black bread or baked (melba-toast-like) thin-sliced bread or crackers.

MAKES ABOUT ½ CUP

JERUSALEM ARTICHOKES (SUNCHOKES)

They were here before we were, and the early American colonists, along with the Indians, knew this plant well. The flavor is smoky and earthy, a bit like potatoes. And the name artichoke is silly, because they're not like the artichoke at all. Actually, they are wild sunflower tubers, often called sunchokes. And they're wonderfully super-crisp and crunchy eaten in the raw, marvelous in any tossed green salad.

Where did the name Jerusalem come from? Originally, the American colonists who came from Spain called them by the Spanish name for sunflower: *girasol* or *girosole,* which became "Jerusalem" as time went by—a simple case of folk etymology.

Shop for fresh ones at a produce market that you can depend on. After sitting about for an inordinate amount of time, they're delicious for cooking only. They look like small sweet potatoes, bumpy and longish and wearing reddish jackets. The flesh inside, however, is pure, gleaming white.

JERUSALEM ARTICHOKES AS IS

Wash them and scrub well with a stiff brush, then peel off the remains of the red skin. Dice or slice in finger-food shapes and serve as is, with a bit of salt or slices of sweet onion.

Note: Once diced, Jerusalem artichokes will keep beautifully in the refrigerator for two weeks immersed in water with a spoonful of lemon juice added.

JERUSALEM ARTICHOKE DICE WITH LAS VEGAS DIP

*4 Jerusalem artichokes, peeled,
    diced, and speared with
    toothpicks
2 ounces blue cheese, mashed
½ cup cream cheese*

*squeeze of lemon juice
quite a bit of freshly ground
    pepper
salt
enough sour cream to soften*

Chill diced artichokes in lemon-water until serving time. Mash the blue cheese with a little of the cream cheese at a time, so it gets well worked in. Mix in the rest of the ingredients. Serve on individual small plates with a dab of the dip, or as a raw vegetable hors d'oeuvre, with the dip in a bowl.

SERVES 4–8

JERUSALEM ARTICHOKES À LA HEALTH-FOOD
RESTAURANT

Small cubes of Jerusalem artichokes in mixed green salads are the very
quintessence of health-food chic. Very trendy, and also very pretty
against the dark greens and the alfalfa sprouts and bacon bits. Their
crunchiness is entrancing to the palate.

1 diced Jerusalem artichoke
almost 1 bunch of spinach leaves
  (very young and fresh, not
  the gigantic ones), torn
a big handful alfalfa sprouts
6 mushrooms, sliced
½ avocado, chunked into dice

1 tablespoon sesame seeds
2 tablespoons sunflower seeds (or
  chopped cashews or wal-
  nuts)
croutons made from 100 percent
  whole-grain bread

VIRGIN DRESSING
½ cup cold-pressed sesame oil
3 tablespoons cider vinegar or
  lemon juice
2 tablespoons freshly grated
  Parmesan cheese
vegetable salt (Veg-it seasoned
  salt or sesame salt, for ex-
  ample)

freshly ground pepper
pinch of brown sugar
1 clove garlic, crushed (optional)

Put vegetables, seeds, and croutons in salad bowl. Mix dressing and
toss.

Many other goodies can be tossed into this salad, so long as they're
fresh: tomato wedges, cucumber slices, bean sprouts, assorted nuts, or
whatever appeals to you.

SERVES 4–8

JICAMA

Once known mainly in Mexico, this crunchy root vegetable is rapidly
becoming a favorite here, and is now available at many markets. It

looks like a very, very large potato, and has a thick skin that peels in a flash. Inside it's white and crunchy, with a slightly applelike sweetness.

Delicious alone, popular with kids, it's now doing the gourmet route at many parties. Good with hot chili dinners. Great with dips and guacamole.

JICAMA STARS

Peel, cut into large thin slices, then cut out with small star cookie cutter. Serve plain or with your favorite dip.

JICAMA, SWISS CHEESE, SALAMI SALAD MEXICANO

If you like Swiss cheese and salami, you'll love this fresh new twist.

> *1½ cups jicama, cut into matchsticks*
> *1 cup Swiss cheese, cut into matchsticks*
> *1 cup salami, cut into matchsticks*
> *⅓ cup oil-and-vinegar dressing*

Toss jicama, cheese, and salami with dressing and chill for an hour or so. Toss again and serve on small iced plates.

SERVES 2–4

LEEKS

Beloved of the French, begotten of the onion family, the lovely white leek, looking as crisp and inviting as celery and resembling a mild-mannered super-scallion, most often winds up in soups and stews.

Now think of the leek also as a salad ingredient of hidden talents. It has a fairly mild flavor, a special tang all its own, but rarely overheats like the brasher onion. In France it is sometimes called the poor man's asparagus, in reference to its flavor when cooked. In early England the leek was loved not only for its taste, both raw and cooked, but for its reputed beneficial effect on health. In still-earlier Roman times, Nero felt the same way.

View it as you would celery, looking for a crisp, fresh appearance. If it is very big and overgrown, it's best for soups. If it's on the young and tender side, buy it for salad.

BABY LEEK RINGS IN MIXED GREENS

Leek rings are wonderful fun in salads. They're like miniature onion rings, pretty and bright with onion flavor.

2 handfuls small romaine leaves, torn

2 handfuls spinach leaves, stems removed

1 medium-size leek, sliced paper-thin crosswise

1 tomato, cut up

1 handful cheese croutons

vinaigrette dressing with hard-cooked egg (see Index)

Prepare salad. Chill. Prepare dressing and let stand. Just before serving, toss together.

SERVES 4

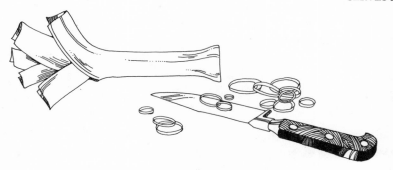

LEEK AND POTATO SALAD

Raw, fresh leeks and cooked cold potatoes go nicely in a light version of potato salad.

½ cup raw leeks, sliced crosswise
    thinly
4 handfuls darker greens
    (spinach, romaine, water-
    cress, curly redleaf lettuce,
    and so on)

2 cups cold boiled potatoes,
    chunked
2 hard-cooked eggs
mayonnaise thinned with sour
    cream
minced parsley

Toss leeks with salad greens and potatoes, and chopped hard-cooked eggs with dressing, just before serving. Or use a plain vinaigrette dressing (see Index) if you prefer.

SERVES 6

MUSHROOMS

Small, medium, or large, they're all divine. Shop for plump, firm mushrooms. If they're shrivelly, pass them by. The price may seem high, but remember that mushrooms are very light in weight as well as light in calories (a mere 12 calories in ½ cup). Wash them gently, thoroughly, and *quickly* in water (they'll soak up water, which dilutes the delicate flavor) just before preparing. Or rub them with a wet paper towel. Store in refrigerator.

EDIBLE WILD MUSHROOMS
Do not confuse cultivated mushrooms at the market with wild mushrooms. While hunting wild mushrooms is a great sport and fascinating for a few, it is also dangerous, since some wild mushrooms are highly poisonous. Do not go mushroom hunting unless you are an expert, or *with* an expert. All in all, the wiser choice is at your market.

SLICED RAW MUSHROOMS
Trim a tiny bit off the bottom of the stems. Then slice them thickly through cap and stem and serve on a dish alone, or with other sliced raw vegetables. Great with dips, too.

STUFFED MUSHROOM CAPS

20 medium or large mushrooms
3 tablespoons finely chopped green onion
salt and pepper to taste
½ cup sour cream or mayonnaise, or a combination of both

Wash mushrooms, which should be very fresh, with gills closed. (A closed-gill mushroom is white on the bottom of the cap and best for raw eating. When the cap underside reveals dark, finely pleated lines, that means the mushroom has dried very slightly, and is preferable for cooking.) Remove stems and chop them very finely, mixing with the onion, salt and pepper, and sour cream or mayonnaise. Salt caps lightly and stuff with mixture. Serve as a side dish, dinner vegetable, or as an hors d'oeuvre.

SERVES 4

WALNUT-STUFFED MUSHROOM CAPS
Very pretty. Stuff each cap with snowy-white sour cream or cream cheese, top each with a walnut half. Save stems for another dish. Allow about 4–6 per person.

CHAMPIGNONS DU MIDI LE MISTRAL
MUSHROOMS IN GARLIC MAYONNAISE (AIOLI)

3 garlic cloves
1 egg yolk
¾ cup olive oil or olive and vege-
  table oil, mixed
dash lemon juice
lukewarm water

salt
½ pound fresh small mushrooms,
  with gills closed
lettuce leaves
chopped parsley for garnish
watercress sprigs (optional)

Make aioli: Crush garlic cloves, or mince finely, and transfer to a bowl. With a wire whisk whip egg yolk into the garlic until the mixture is well blended and light. Pour the oil in very slowly, drop by drop, whisking the mixture constantly until the sauce is thickened and smooth. (If you have no wire whisk, use an eggbeater.) Add a dash or two of lemon juice, a little lukewarm water, and salt to taste.

(To make aioli in a blender, crush or press garlic cloves, put in blender with egg yolk, and slowly dribble in the oil as you blend at low speed.)

Wipe mushrooms with a damp cloth, cut each mushroom into 4 slices, and very gently mix them into the aioli sauce. Arrange on lettuce leaves; top with a little chopped parsley and maybe a few sprigs of watercress. Serve the mushrooms as an appetizer or as a dinner salad.

SERVES 4

PARSLEY

One morning in the garden bed
The onion and the carrot said
Unto the parsley group:
"Oh, when shall we three meet again—
in thunder, lightning, or in rain?"
"Alas," replied in tones of pain
The parsley, "in the soup."
—C. S. CALVERLY

Why oh why is the parsley always stuck in the soup? Its only alternative is to languish as a garnish, more often thrown away than not after the meal. Pity the parsley, the victim of its curly green beauty.

Parsley should be eaten, for it tastes good and is simply bursting with Vitamin A and Vitamin C, among other nutrients: great for your eyes, your teeth, your skin.

HOW TO BUY PARSLEY AND STORE IT IN A VASE

Buy stiff, perky bundles of parsley that look fluffy and firm or try the flat-leafed Italian parsley. Rinse off and store in water, in a tall glass or small vase, in the refrigerator. It's as pretty as a bunch of flowers; put it on an eye-level shelf so you'll notice its beauty every time you open the refrigerator door.

THE TRICK TO RELEASING PARSLEY FLAVOR

Grinding or very finely mincing, then crushing parsley is the best way to serve it on foods. This releases the volatile nutrients that are tightly held in the curly parsley leaves, and the fresh flavor.

PARSLEY WITH ROQUEFORT OR BLUE CHEESE DIP

Chilled parsley is fun to munch on, and tastes marvelous with dips. It's also incredibly quick and easy to prepare.

> *2 bunches parsley flowerets, chilled, with stalks cut short*
> *1 cup Roquefort or blue cheese dip (see Index or use your own)*

Arrange brilliant green flowerets on a plate around creamy dip and serve. Each person holds floweret by the stalk, dips in sauce, and eats.

SERVES 6

PARSLEY BUTTER

> *1 stick butter*
> *1 teaspoon or more lemon juice*
> *salt and pepper (just a bit)*
> *3 tablespoons finely minced fresh parsley*

Soften the butter (if you use unsalted butter, a bit more salt will be needed) and cream with lemon juice and salt and pepper. Now mash in vigorously the chopped parsley. Let stand in the refrigerator. Use just as you would plain butter (it's especially delicious on cooked vegetables and fish). It will keep at least a week or 10 days.

PARSLEY, GIVER OF SWEET BREATH

Parsley lets you gobble garlic incognito. It clears the palate after a garlic dish, and is eaten in this fashion traditionally in many European countries that revere garlic.

Hail, parsley. It's even cheap and low-calorie.

PEAS

Green peas come 4 to 7 peas in a beautiful smooth green pod. One pound of peas in the pod yields approximately 2 cups of peas. The pods are a snap to open: Just press the narrow end and a split appears; zip it open with your finger. When you shop, open one pod and taste a raw pea. If it's sweet, the peas are nice and fresh and young—perfect for eating raw. If it's not sweet, the peas are fresh but quite mature, and need to be cooked.

Beautiful Peas in the Pod

Serve the peas in the pod, heaped on a platter, or in a shallow salad bowl. Everyone will open the pods and eat the peas out of hand, enjoying himself immensely. The taste is heavenly, sweet and crunchy.

For adults this is novel cocktail food. For children it's like eating candy, since young peas, after all, are loaded with natural sugar.

Peas in a Nut Dish

Shelled green peas can be served as a snack or an hors d'oeuvre in a pretty silver nut dish or small candy dish. They'll go faster than peanuts.

PEAS IN SALAD

Toss shelled peas in practically any salad. They're especially nice in a tossed green salad with onion. Add a few orange sections and it's glorious.

PEELED PEA PODS

A novelty worth trying. As farm children have done for generations, your children (and you) will enjoy peeling the green part of the pea pod away from the transparent part of the pod "skin." The green part is simply delicious, though of course you must have the time and the patience of a pomegranate eater.

SNOW PEAS (ORIENTAL OR CHINESE PEA PODS)

Exquisite—and so expensive they should be served a few at a time, with a dip or in a salad.

SNOW PEA AND MUSHROOM SALAD

A lovely side dish at any dinner—good with roasts, chicken, pork.

> *¼ pound snow peas*
> *¼ pound mushrooms, thinly sliced*
> *¼ cup Chinese sesame-soy dressing*

CHINESE SESAME-SOY DRESSING

> *4 teaspoons soy sauce*
> *1 teaspoon sugar*
> *2 teaspoons sesame seed oil*

Mix together until sugar is completely dissolved. Toss chilled salad in dressing. Serve immediately or chill for 2–3 hours.

SERVES 4

POTATOES IN THE RAW

The devotees of raw potatoes are not yet numerous, but they are ardent. Once you have acquired a taste for sliced raw potatoes, it can be a craving when you see a nice young-looking new potato. Try them occasionally with your assorted raw vegetables. With a dip or without, they have a super-crunchiness that is most refreshing.

Select only new potatoes. All the big baking potatoes are best for baking, as they taste too musty raw. Children are fond of raw potatoes, which are, of course, more nutritious than the cooked variety. Once I turned my back on my eighteen-month-old who was sitting in a supermarket cart. When I turned back, he was about halfway through eating a potato, which he had lifted from the cart while passers-by gaped in horror. I took the potato away, because it needed peeling, and explained to the audience that it was actually quite good for him. They quite obviously thought I was demented, so I slunk away, while my baby cried in outrage at his loss.

NAKED, BEAUTIFUL POTATOES
Peel and wash new potatoes. Slice them, dip them in very icy water, and serve fanned out on a small platter, garnished with parsley or with other raw vegetables. Seasoned salt is optional. Good with all the raw-vegetable dips.

NOTES ON PREPARING POTATOES
If you're not sure which is a new potato, talk to the produce man. Peel and slice your potatoes *just before serving* or immerse in water until ready to use. Remember that sliced potatoes turn brown, like apples, if you leave them out for more than a few minutes.

FRENCH UNFRIES

3 potatoes, very fresh

Chill potatoes until icy-cold. Just before serving, peel, wash, and slice into French-fry sticks (nice with a zigzag potato cutter). Serve on a small plate, dip in a little bowl of . . . what else? cold ketchup! Or heap on a checkered napkin in a rustic basket with other raw vegetables.

SERVES 4

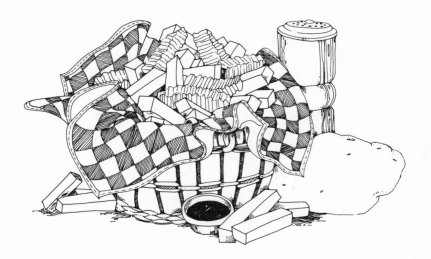

ONIONS

MARINATED ONIONS

If you are fortunate enough to have a source of sweet rather than sharp onions, these are delicious marinated in oil-and-vinegar dressing for several hours.

SPROUTS

DELICATE ALFALFA SPROUTS SALAD

Inspired by the Prairie Salad at Señor Pico's.

2 cups packed alfalfa sprouts
oil-and-vinegar dressing

It's embarrassingly simple. Fluff the alfalfa sprouts with your fingers, toss with dressing, add salt and pepper if you wish.

SERVES 4

ALFALFA SPROUTS VINAIGRETTE WITH EGG

Alfalfa sprouts and a mild salad dressing have a beautiful way of complementing each other. The simpler, the better.

2 cups alfalfa sprouts
1 hard-cooked egg, minced (optional)
¼ cup vinaigrette dressing (see Index)

Toss sprouts and egg in dressing, making sure that all the slender sprouts are covered lightly. Serve on icy-cold salad plates.

SERVES 2–4

CHOO SOOK NA MOOL
KOREAN BEAN SPROUT SALAD

4 cups bean sprouts
1 green pepper, chopped
8 green onions, chopped
1 tomato, chopped

sesame-soy dressing (4 tablespoons soy
sauce, 1 tablespoon sugar, and 2
tablespoons sesame seed oil, stirred
until sugar dissolves)

This salad can be prepared with varying quantities of ingredients. The

Korean way is mostly sprouts, with small amounts of other vegetables, giving it a very pretty confetti look. You can also make the salad with more tomato and reduce the quantity of sprouts.

This salad can be tossed with its dressing before dinner, then chilled in refrigerator until serving time. It will even keep overnight, though it will not be as pretty and fresh looking the next day. Serve with any meal you would serve a green salad with. It's delicious with grilled meats and fish, broiled chicken, fried foods, ribs. Even a simple grilled hotdog looks smashing with this colorful salad beside it. For parties, it makes a magnificent buffet display. And don't you like the name? Choo Sook Na Mool . . .

SERVES 4

STRING BEANS

"Name some really unusual raw food," I begged my friend Carolyn.

"I don't *know* any," she cried, "I don't know a single unusual one. Only just the ordinary things like celery and carrot sticks and string beans—"

"String beans?"

"Stupid," Carolyn said kindly, "everyone anywhere eats raw string beans."

"Well, I never heard of it, and I've heard of a lot of foods . . ."

"You're a city kid, that's all. If you had grown up on a farm you'd have eaten tons of string beans and corn right from the fields. Everyone does."

So I ate a raw string bean, and I liked it. Very chewy and fun to munch on.

Raw string beans, fresh and young (not gnarled and huge), are a handsome addition to your raw-vegetable platters and green salads. If the string beans are relatively unmarked and do not have lumps where the little beans inside show, and they are a fresh-looking green, then they're good for eating in the raw.

EATING STRING BEANS IN THE RAW

Just rinse off the string beans, break off the little tips at either end, and serve with seasoned salt or plain salt. Or with nothing at all.

STRING BEANS WITH BLUE CHEESE DIP

Delicious. For their striking appearance they belong on the most elaborate raw-vegetable platters. Some people go wild over them, some demur. But they are always a conversation piece. (For dip see Index.)

MINUTE-BLANCHED STRING BEANS

Not quite so crispy, but a more brilliant green. Dip the string beans into a pot of boiling water for 1 minute. Quickly remove and plunge into icy-cold water for 2 minutes. Then chill and serve. Or marinate them, as in following recipe.

VEIDA'S DILL-MARINATED STRING BEANS

8 tablespoons soy oil
2 tablespoons wine or cider vinegar
1 scant teaspoon dry mustard
1 teaspoon sugar
1 teaspoon dried dill weed, crushed (or several small sprigs, or 1 long stalk fresh dill, chopped and crushed with the back of a spoon)

1 clove garlic, pressed or minced
1 pound string beans

Mix dressing-marinade. Blanch string beans as described above and toss in the dressing mixture. Marinate in the refrigerator for an hour or a day, depending on how you like the marinade to penetrate. They're good after an hour, but sharper the next day. They'll keep for several days, so save a few to throw in your next tossed green salad.

SERVES 6–8

SUMMER SQUASH

Winter squashes—butternut, Hubbard, and acorn, to name a few—can be eaten in the raw in thin sticks for dipping, or grated in salads, but they may be too tough for some palates.

The summer squashes are quite another story. Smaller, prettier, shaded in different colors, they are quite tender and lovely, and so delicious raw that you should eat them that way a good part of the time.

The best-known are zucchini (the most famous), yellow crookneck squash, the pale-green, scallop-shaped flower that is called summer squash, and chayote.

Incidentally, if you happen to grow your own, squash flowers, the brilliant blooms that precede each squash, are delicious on top of salads. And they look gorgeous.

POSH SQUASH SALAD MARINATED IN WINE AND DILL

1 zucchini
1 yellow crookneck squash
1 summer squash
10 cherry tomatoes
10 black olives
½ chopped onion

large handful grated cheddar or Jack cheese
5 sliced mushrooms (optional)
2 tablespoons minced, crushed parsley
1 head romaine lettuce

DRESSING

3 tablespoons red wine vinegar
2 tablespoons red or white wine
1 clove garlic, crushed
salt

pepper
¼–½ teaspoon crushed dried dill
¼ teaspoon dry mustard
½ cup salad oil or safflower oil

Cut up squash into bite-size pieces, slicing zucchini and yellow squash crosswise and cutting summer squash into small wedges. Mix dressing, adding oil last, and toss all salad ingredients in it. Cover and marinate

8–12 hours, tossing occasionally in marinade if convenient. Serve on romaine leaves, halved.

SERVES 4–6

SUMMER SQUASH IN BAGNA CAUDA

Assorted squashes are particularly attractive for a simple version of bagna cauda (see Index), the Italian hot-oil-with-anchovies dip.

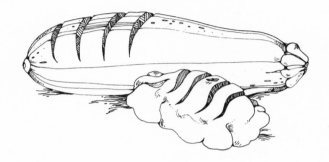

ASSORTED SQUASH SPEARS WITH GUACAMOLE

Guacamole with mayonnaise added (see Index) goes beautifully with zucchini. Just cut the zucchini lengthwise into quarters, and then once or twice crosswise. Spoon guacamole on top of each serving. This makes a nice side dish when you're serving a simple casserole for supper.

SUMMER-SQUASH "CRACKERS"

With any spread that tastes good on crackers, try the fresh (and lower-calorie) idea of pale-green flower-shaped summer squash, cut horizontally into elegant flower slices, as a cracker substitute.

ZUCCHINI

This long, dark, and handsome squash is so easily grown, so easily cooked, and so popular that we often don't think of it as a raw vegetable.

But that's all changing, and raw zucchini is rapidly moving up to reign with the celery stalk on vegetable platters.

Consider this: zucchini is available in all seasons, and it's the easiest raw vegetable of all to prepare—you just wash and quarter lengthwise, then cut into two or three sections, and *voilà!*—you have 8 or 12 dippers per zucchini. No peeling, crisping, scrubbing, virtually no wilting. And precious few calories!

The flavor of zucchini does beautiful things with dips. It's just bland enough to show off the character of each dip beautifully. To name a few . . .

ZUCCHINI WITH TOMATO DIP
Ever the friend of the tomato, as in cooked zucchini dishes, so it is with the raw version. Try the tomato dip on page 163.

ZUCCHINI WITH PLAIN MAYONNAISE
The neglected plain mayonnaise dip comes into its own with zucchini. Make your own mayonnaise (see Index). It's more elegant, and it's also cheaper.

ZUCCHINI WITH AVOCADO DIP
From guacamole to avocado mashed with mayonnaise and a little lemon, all avocado dips taste heavenly with zucchini.

FAT ZUCCHINI CRACKERS
Whenever you see really fat zucchini at the market, snap them up to cut into "crackers." Serve them with any spread you would serve on a regular cracker.

ZUCCHINI SLICED INTO SALAD
Every respectable salad bin has a zucchini or two waiting to be sliced into the evening salad. For eye appeal alone, every salad deserves zucchini.

MARINATED ZUCCHINI, ONION, AND TOMATO

> *1 large zucchini*
> *1 large tomato*
> *1 large onion*
> *¾–1 cup oil-and-vinegar dressing*

Slice the zucchini, tomato, and onion onto a shallow dish, pour on the dressing, and marinate for at least an hour, tumbling occasionally. Serve as is or with a sprinkling of Parmesan cheese, or toss in a salad bowl with romaine leaves.

SERVES 4

CHAYOTE

CHAYOTE SQUASH STICKS

Mmm. A super-crunchy cucumber masquerading as a squash? Chayote, while it looks like a faded green pepper, is a squash that is showing up in more and more markets, sometimes called custard marrow or vegetable pear. Peel it, and the inside is a dazzlingly pale, cool, translucent cucumber color. It's marvelous with dips, lovely just dunked in sour cream, and an engaging new conversation piece for your raw-vegetable repertoire. Cucumber eaters will enjoy it. Try serving it with blue-cheese dip.

TOMATOES

Creating the perfect tomato dish is something that starts in the earth, for outstanding seed, nurtured soil, sun-ripening and vine-ripening have a lot to do with it. Many a true tomato buff who has not found a good source of fine local tomatoes takes to his own garden, for good tomatoes can be surprisingly easy to grow in some climates. A market that earnestly tries to stock tasty tomatoes is well worth patronizing.

WESLEY'S TOMATO: THE LOVE APPLE

Once having found the ideal tomato, Wesley argues, one that is bursting with red, ripe, tomato-y flavor, it is superfluous to fuss with it. Eat it raw and it is truly the "love apple" that was its original name. Each bite should be followed by a sprinkling of salt. The tomato has more flavor at room temperature, but a chilled one is very appealing on a hot summer afternoon.

TOMATOES WITH HEARTS OF PALM

If good, ripe tomatoes are available, this is an elegant way to serve them.

4 tomatoes, peeled and sliced thickly
1 can (4–8 ounces) hearts of palm
1 hard-cooked egg, chopped fine
2 tablespoons parsley, minced very fine
¾ cup vinaigrette dressing (see Index)

Arrange tomato slices on individual serving plates. Chop chilled hearts of palm into rather large pieces, and marinate with egg and parsley in vinaigrette dressing for about 20 minutes. Spoon over tomato slices, making sure dressing covers tomatoes well. Serve immediately or chill until dinner. Black olives can be added for garnish.

SERVES 4

PEELED CHERRY TOMATO SALAD

This charming salad is a tender, piquant combination of marinated cherry tomatoes that have been peeled (don't panic, it's quite simple) and fat young mushrooms. It is served on a bed of watercress as an appetizer course—or heaped in a glass snifter or bowl, to be passed with toothpicks and napkins as an hors d'oeuvre.

1 box (about ¾–1 pound)
cherry tomatoes
½–⅔ pound fat small mush-
rooms, gills closed (or
larger ones cut in halves
or thirds)

1 teaspoon minced basil
¾ cup oil-and-vinegar dressing
1 large bunch watercress or other
greens

Pour tomatoes into a pot of boiling water, let stand for 30 seconds, then remove to a pot of ice-cold water. Skins will then peel off easily. Wash and trim bottom of mushroom stems. Mix a small amount of basil with dressing and pour over tomatoes and mushrooms in bowl; let marinate for at least 4 hours, or all day. Before serving, taste and add a bit more salt or freshly ground pepper if needed. Sprinkle remaining basil on tomatoes and mushrooms and serve on individual watercress beds on small plates. Use any leftover marinade for salad dressing.

SERVES 4–6

TOMATESOV SALATA
ARMENIAN TOMATO SALAD

This salad was originally designed to go with Chi Kufta (see page 71). It is also fine just as a dinner salad. Or heaped on pita bread. Or served with steak tartare.

2 large onions
salt to taste
6 large ripe, firm tomatoes

1 large green pepper
1 cup chopped parsley
oil-and-vinegar dressing to taste

Slice onions and put in salad bowl. Sprinkle generously with salt. Then crush onions and salt continually with heel of your hand until onion juices are released. Rinse hands. Cut tomatoes bite-size and add to onions. Slice green pepper into mixture. Add parsley and toss all together a little. Finally, season to taste with salt and dressing.

SERVES 6–8

Note: Unlike green salads, this one will keep overnight in the refrigerator and taste good next day. If you just have a little left over, toss into tomorrow's mixed green salad for a refreshing tang of marinated onion and tomato.

CHERRY TOMATOES, BROCCOLI FLOWERS, CUCUMBER CUBES
Spear broccoli flowerets, cucumber cubes, and cherry tomatoes, on big toothpicks for dipping. Or just gather on a plate. They make a very striking mix of colors and shapes. Try them with plain mayonnaise or your favorite dip.

STUFFED CHERRY TOMATOES
Salt cavity after you hollow out with little knife. Stuff with cream cheese mashed with Roquefort cheese. Top each with a single caper or anchovy bit.

GUACAMOLE STUFFED TOMATOES

This is a strikingly pretty addition to a lunch or dinner salad course. If you're being quite formal, peel the tomatoes first. Otherwise, it's not at all necessary.

1 large avocado, peeled and mashed
2 tablespoons finely minced onion
⅛ teaspoon seasoned salt (or more to taste)
3–4 drops Tabasco Sauce
½–¾ teaspoon lemon juice

⅓ cup peeled, seeded, and minced cucumber (optional)
6 small or medium size ripe tomatoes, chilled
3 tablespoons cheddar cheese, grated (optional)

Keep tomatoes in refrigerator till ready to serve. Mix all ingredients together except for cheddar cheese, which is a garnish. Taste and add more lemon if a slight tang is wished—be careful not to let the lemon overpower the subtle richness of the dip. Add more salt if necessary. Immerse avocado pit in mixture if dish is prepared ahead of serving, to keep dip green. Just before serving, place tomatoes on individual serving plates. Slice each tomato from the top to within ½ inch of the bottom, making a cross. Slice down again twice, in between the first cross-sections, making 8 almost-sliced-through sections. Press gently apart to make a flower petal effect. Heap guacamole into the center of each tomato. Sprinkle with cheese if wished.

SERVES 6

Note: some people prefer guacamole with mayonnaise added. While it is not the authentic recipe, if you prefer it, add 2 tablespoons to the mix.

TURNIPS

At almost every market there's a crunchy, surprisingly sweet surprise: the turnip. When you cook turnips their natural sugars turn to starch, so why cook? Look for small or medium turnips. Avoid huge ones that look as if they've been stored a long time. They should be super-firm.

Just peel and slice them, chill, and arrange on a dark platter or wooden slab in a decorative pattern. Fresh and snowy, tantalizingly different . . . your friends will wonder what they *are.* Don't tell them. Put them out with carrot sticks and raw mushroom caps, or curled green onion and slivered cauliflowerets. The only people who will guess what they are will already be raw-turnip fans. No dip is needed, as fresh turnips have a tingly, naturally sweet flavor, very crispy and delightful.

A CHILD'S GARDEN OF TURNIPS
Cut the turnips in amusing shapes—diamonds, blocks, snipped slices with pinking shears—and serve them to children, who instantly love their sweetness.

SALAD GREENS

Mixed greens, varied by the season, by your mood, tossed with casual confidence, gleaming with dressing—crispy and beautiful, they're the happiest of eating, for there is nothing more delicious than the simple, classic unadorned salad of mixed greens.

Tear the leaves into fairly large pieces. Do not cut the very leafy greens, just rip with your fingers. Greens should be cut only when you want a chiffonade-type salad (thin ribbons of green).

Properly, you should quickly rinse full leaves in cold water in your sink as soon as you get home from the market. Then shake and pop into refrigerator in sealed plastic bags when they're fairly dry—drippy greens wilt, and don't hold salad dressing. If you don't have time to dry greens well, pat with a paper or cloth towel to absorb extra moisture. They'll keep in your greens bin for 2–7 days, depending on the freshness and fragility of the particular green. Don't throw out wilted greens—throw them into your blender, and then add them to soup broths.

Greens for salads must be fresh. Freshness is the key to success. The French understand this very well, and thus their salad recipes are justly legendary.

VARY YOUR GREENS

As the seasons change, your market displays some glorious fresh greens that are delightfully easy to include in your favorite green salads. Try to stay out of a too-lengthy one-green rut, no matter how pleasant. Experiment. It's deliciously easy and failsafe, because virtually all greens are enhanced by salad dressings.

Have you explored the various lettuces lately? These would include bibb (limestone), butter (Boston), iceberg (the traditional), Kentucky, and the enchanting redleaf. Actually, they're *all* enchanting!

Then there are the romaine-like lettuces—American endive and escarole.

And those sometimes delicate, sometimes hearty cabbage variations like bok choy, Chinese cabbage, coriander cabbage, red cabbage, Brussels sprouts (the last two are discussed on pages 112–114).

And then the old-fashioned, and now very newly fashionable, spinach, too rich in acids to be served every single day, but an excellent salad base served moderately.

The peppery greens, with a slightly bitter flavor, have a special appeal: parsley and chicory (cicoria).

And the divine watercress.

Give your favorite greens a piquant new look by adding a few off-beat greens like fennel, bok choy, very young nasturtium leaves, very young and fresh dandelion leaves, old-country sorrel greens (sour leaves), purslane, beet greens, and dock.

Beauty and health note: The truly dark greens are the millionaires of the Vitamin A family. Healthy, beautiful skin and bright eyes are just two of the reasons why Vitamin A is more than simply gourmet.

Wherever you live, there are local greens with a special taste appeal, just waiting to be chilled and tossed in even the simplest salad dressing, and prized for their delectable freshness. Ask the produce man, who will often have a delicious serving suggestion.

OCCASIONAL GREENS
Turnip greens, beet greens, and spinach are good raw, great in salads and rich in nutrients, but they should be eaten raw in moderate quantities. They contain a small amount of oxalic acid, which if eaten in large quantities tends briefly to reduce our body's ability to absorb needed calcium. So think of these as "rich" greens that you should eat and enjoy, but not daily.

CHICORY—THE WILD ENDIVE

Mama mia, cicoria!

This curly green-and-white salad green with a slightly bitter but habit-forming appeal is a traditional salad green in France and Italy, which is now growing in popularity as a favored American green.

Because it has lusty character to its flavor, chicory lends itself well to savory salads with meats and cheeses, or tuna fish or anchovies. Chicory's wry, sardonic crispness stands up to strong cheese and savory tastes, where a more delicate green would simply wilt and faint away.

CHICORY-DICKORY-DOCK
SALAD WITH HONEYED DRESSING

Since there's a bit of bitterness in every bite of chicory greens, this salad turns it into fun by adding a specially sweet tasting dressing. For children, you might want to do something silly like cutting up pieces of cucumber in the vague shape of a tiny white mouse. As you get to know chicory, you'll find other salad ingredients you love to combine with it.

1 head chicory
dock leaves (optional)
1 cucumber, cut into crescents
oil-and-vinegar dressing with 2
    teaspoons honey added

¾ cup butter or cheese croutons
grated Parmesan cheese

Cut off bottom of chicory; separate and wash leaves. Drain on towel. Wash dock leaves and drain on towel. Peel cucumber, halve, and scoop out seeds. Slice crosswise into thick crescents. Pour dressing on salad in bowl just before serving and toss well. Add croutons and grated cheese at the very end, and toss gently.

SERVES 4–6

DANDELION GREENS

A century ago dandelion greens were an early-spring treat. Today they're a favorite of the eating-in-the-wild crowd. The folk-medicine buffs impute all sorts of vigorous benefits to them. And in Italy they are held in esteem in the traditional cuisine of Italian mixed green salads.

They are available at some markets in the spring and early summer, and wild in lawns and fields (if they haven't been sprayed with garden chemicals). The young spring leaves are sumptuous in a salad. Skip the bitter older leaves. Treat them just as you would any salad green, rinsing quickly, patting dry, keeping in plastic bags in the salad bin of your refrigerator.

Long before nutritionists analyzed a dandelion leaf and discovered it was a splendid source of Vitamin A (over 15,000 units of A in 1 cup of greens, a tremendous amount), people knew they lost that "poorly" feeling when this and other spring greens appeared on their salad plates. But the flavor of dandelion greens is the best reason for including them in your salads; slightly tangy, slightly rich, they add a tingling touch of freshness.

YOUR FIRST DANDELION GREENS
Just toss a few of them into one of your regular mixed salads. Don't shock the unwary with a big bowl of dandelion greens all at once. After you're a dandelion devotee, try this Italian salad—the essence of simplicity, and beautiful, too.

INSALATA DI CICORIA FINA
DANDELION SALAD

This a simple toss of dandelion leaves and black olives; you can add a few radishes for color. For drama's sake, top salad with a yellow dandelion flower.

> *1 handful dandelion greens per person*
> *4 ripe olives per person*
> *oil-and-vinegar dressing*

Chill dandelion leaves. Tear and toss with olives, adding sliced radishes if you wish. Or sprinkle with sesame seeds.

INSALATA MISTA CON CICORIA
SALAD MIXED WITH DANDELION GREENS

½ head escarole
½ head chicory (wild endive)
¼ pound (a few handfuls) dandelion greens
½ medium cucumber, peeled and sliced

ITALIAN BASIL DRESSING

½ cup olive oil or salad oil

4 tablespoons wine or cider vinegar

3 tablespoons chopped fresh basil, or
2 teaspoons dried basil

1 clove or more garlic, crushed
or pressed

salt and freshly ground pepper

Wash, dry, and chill greens. Peel and slice cucumber. Tear greens into wooden salad bowl and refrigerate, covered, until just before serving. Mix dressing and let it sit at room temperature for a few hours to develop the basil flavor (or keep in refrigerator overnight). Toss greens in dressing.

SERVES 6–8

FENNEL

INSALATA DI FINOCCHIO, POMODORO, E CICORIA
FENNEL, TOMATO, AND CHICORY SALAD

1 head fennel (finocchio)

1 small head chicory

2 large ripe tomatoes

1–2 cloves garlic, minced

salt and pepper to taste

2 tablespoons wine vinegar

6 tablespoons olive oil (or safflower or
vegetable/soy oil)

Remove any outer leaves from fennel and chicory. Wash under running water, cut off bottoms. Tear chicory into pieces and place on absorbent paper or a clean kitchen towel to drain thoroughly. Cut fennel into thin slices. Quarter tomatoes, or cut them in sixths or eighths if you prefer, and set aside.

In a cup, mix garlic and salt and pepper with vinegar to dissolve salt. Add oil and blend well. Just before serving, pour dressing on fennel, tomatoes, and chicory, which you have heaped into salad bowl, and toss vigorously. Taste for seasoning. If you wish, fennel can be mixed with salad dressing, then refrigerated to marinate very briefly, say 5 minutes. Then fennel and dressing can be added to salad and tossed at table.

SERVES 6–8

LETTUCE

BOSTON CREAM SALAD

This is a tender creamy salad that lets the soft, silky Boston lettuce solo. Use it also for the other small, less crunchy lettuces like bibb lettuce, butter lettuce, limestone lettuce.

Boston lettuce	*pepper*
4 hard-cooked egg yolks	*2 or more tablespoons lemon juice*
1 cup heavy cream	*parsley (optional)*
½ teaspoon or less salt	

Wash and dry lettuce leaves and tear into quite large pieces. Chill. Mash the egg yolks into a little of the cream. Add remaining ingredients (except parsley), stirring the lemon juice in very gradually so it won't separate from the cream. Gently toss dressing and salad just before serving. Sprinkle minced parsley on top. Serve on chilled plates as a separate salad course with hot tiny rolls, or halved refrigerator rolls that you have rolled in a generous amount of poppy or sesame seeds before baking. Soft hot breads go nicely with the creamy dressing and the delicate flavor of these softer salad greens.

SERVES 4–6

A FEW PERFECT ROMAINE LEAVES SALAD

This salad was inspired by Ernie's, a restaurant in San Francisco, where I first enjoyed the immaculate panache of plain chilled perfect inner romaine leaves, fresh and crisp, with only a vinaigrette dressing poured on top. Leaves are served whole.

> *1 head romaine*
> *⅓ cup vinaigrette dressing (see Index)*
> *1 minced hard-cooked egg*
> *1 tablespoon minced parsley*

Use only the inner half of romaine, and do not tear. Serve separate whole leaves, tumbled very carefully in dressing. Pour rest of dressing and egg on arranged leaves on individual plates and garnish with parsley. Chill plates and forks in freezer. Be sure romaine is very fresh and crisp and cold. Superb!

SERVES 4

ROMAINE SALAD WITH GORGONZOLA DRESSING

> *1 large head romaine*
> *1 sweet onion, sliced*

GORGONZOLA DRESSING

¼ teaspoon dry mustard, moistened with a little water
salt and pepper
1 garlic clove, minced

2 tablespoons wine vinegar
6 tablespoons olive, soy, or safflower oil
1½ ounces Gorgonzola cheese

Wash and dry romaine, reserving the outermost leaves for another salad. Tear inner leaves into bowl and add onion. Mix mustard, salt and pepper, garlic, and vinegar and stir vigorously. Add oil and blend well. Add crumbled Gorgonzola cheese and mix thoroughly. If this dressing stands for a few hours at room temperature it will develop its cheese flavor more enticingly. Cheese salad dressings, like cheeses themselves, are best at room temperature. Chilling blunts their flavor. Toss salad with dressing at table. This is a refreshing change from blue and Roquefort dressings.

SERVES 4–6

WATERCRESS

The delicate, peppery freshness of watercress has made it a favorite in many cuisines. Watercress is cultivated, as its name implies, close to water. Look for dark-green unwilted bunches at the market. Take it home, wash, and refrigerate, loosely wrapped. Bunches are easily cut off at the base in one stroke at serving time. But enjoy it soon. Cress will fade and wilt quickly—and with that rich green color goes the fantastic richness of Vitamin A. Calories? About 12 for a whole bunch.

WATERCRESS SALAD WITH WALNUTS AND TURKEY

Make a small salad for each person.

*2 bunches watercress, torn into
    pieces
¼ cup chopped celery
2 slices crisp bacon, crumbled
    (optional)
¼ cup walnut halves*

*6 slices (about 6 ounces) cold
    cooked turkey, cut into
    slivers
oil-and-vinegar dressing with dash
    of sugar*

Slice off watercress stems in one cut before you untie bunch. Wash and shake dry, drain on paper towel, and chill. Toss watercress, celery, bacon, walnuts, and turkey in the dressing just before serving. Taste for seasoning, add more salt and pepper, and make sure dressing is not too tart.

SERVES 4

Note: Other nuts (cashews, pecans, chestnuts) of all kinds may be substituted for the walnuts with delicious results.

SALAD DRESSINGS

Many excellent salad dressings are listed elsewhere, with specific recipes. By all means, use these dressings (see Index for each) with lots of other salads: *Gorgonzola dressing* (good enough to make blue cheese turn green with envy), *basil dressing, poppy-seed dressing, salsa fria,* and many more.

VINAIGRETTE DRESSING
THE CLASSIC FRENCH WAY

The classic vinaigrette is austerely simple. There are thousands of variations, and who can resist them? But don't forget the original. It is generally one part vinegar to two parts of oil. Reducing the vinegar

makes a blander, more subtle dressing. Increasing the vinegar proportions makes a dressing with more bite.

> *1 ounce vinegar*
> *3 ounces good light olive oil or salad oil*
> *¼ teaspoon salt*
> *⅛ teaspoon pepper, freshly ground*

Stir together vigorously with a fork. Toss with salad just before serving
if leafy greens are used (otherwise the salt will draw moisture from
the greens and make them wilt). Taste a salad leaf, and add more salt
or vinegar if needed. Serve on mixed greens or other salad ingredients.
A large handful of greens is usually sufficient per person.

SERVES 4

Vinaigrette Dressing with Garlic and Mustard
To many people, this is the preferred classic. Add 1 or 2 chopped garlic
cloves (not crushed) and ¼ teaspoon dry mustard or ½ teaspoon
Grey Poupon mustard to the vinaigrette dressing above.

Vinaigrette Dressing Variations
The ways of a good vinaigrette are wondrous and mysterious. The
additions are infinite, and up to you. Fresh or dried herbs and spices.
Grated Parmesan and Romano cheese, or any grated cheese. Vinaigrette
is marinated in chopped fresh tomato before tossing. Start mixing the
dressing with a base of 1 egg yolk (raw). Chill the dressing overnight.
Crush the garlic with the salt first.

Which oil? To each his own favorite. I prefer a mix of soy or safflower oil, vegetable oil, and light olive oil. Next year I may change my
mind. Some add a little white wine. Some swear by a pinch of sugar
or honey in dressings.

Which vinegar? Try some different vinegars, but don't neglect
simple cider vinegar, white tarragon vinegar, red wine vinegar. Do not
use white vinegar. Some gourmet markets and restaurants have their
own special local brands, which are often superb.

If you are fortunate enough to have fresh herbs growing in your kitchen garden, by all means chop these finely and mix in for a superb dressing.

HARD-COOKED EGG: THE DRESSING SAVER

Sometimes a dressing just won't come together. Your experiment went a bit awry, or the weather isn't right. Keep a hard-cooked egg handy to chop and stir into these dressings, and it will magically blend the flavors together divinely. No refrigerator should be without this last-minute gourmet trick.

GREEN GODDESS DRESSING

This is a magnificent dressing. It is especially brilliant on salads that are fairly rich, hearty salads with some crunchy tangy ingredients. Chef's salads, salads with some cut-up root vegetables and cabbage mixed in with the greens. Salads with bits of spicy pepper and onion, peppery greens like chicory and the dark greens and watercress.

½ cup heavy cream
1 tablespoon lemon juice
1 cup mayonnaise
1 generous tablespoon anchovy paste
5 tablespoons tarragon vinegar

½ cup or more minced green onion
⅓ cup parsley, minced very finely

Mix all together and shake. Let stand for at least 1 hour. Pour over salad just before serving and toss.

The blender version is easier. Just pop all into the blender (don't bother mincing parsley or onion) and whirl until smooth. Let stand for at least 1 hour.

SERVES 6–8

Note: Green Goddess Dressing is named for its color, which is a particularly cool and fetching shade of pale green.

GRAHAM'S
BLUE CHEESE BUTTERMILK DRESSING

Buttermilk is a delicious and low-calorie alternative to oil and vinegar in some dressings. It has the tang of a light vinegar, and the silkiness of oil. It also carries other flavors well.

Graham is a thirteen-year-old uninhibited dressing maker, and comes up with some inspired dressings, usually by adding "something."

½ cup buttermilk   4 ounces blue cheese
¼ cup mayonnaise   ¼ cup chopped parsley
½ cup sour cream

Blend all in blender. If too rich, add more buttermilk. Leaving out salt and pepper enhances the cheesy flavor.

SERVES 4–6

ROQUEFORT DRESSING WITH SOUR CREAM

⅛ cup milk
1 tablespoon oil
3 ounces Roquefort cheese
¾ cup sour cream

Blend everything but sour cream in blender. Add sour cream, and blend again. Season with salt and pepper only if preferred.

SERVES 4

AIOLI
GARLIC MAYONNAISE

In Spain, the mayonnaise that reigns is plainly marvelous. It's the garlic, of course—even timid garlic users are charmed—and an elegant simplicity. Aioli should be accompanied with sprigs of parsley as a chaser, for those who wish to instantly freshen their breath.

8 cloves garlic, peeled

1 large egg yolk

¼ teaspoon salt

pinch pepper

3–4 tablespoons good light olive
    oil (such as Bertoli)

1 cup olive oil (or half olive, half
    vegetable oil)

juice of ½ lemon

1 tablespoon ice water

Put garlic, egg yolk, salt, and pepper in blender. Blend at high speed until good and foamy. Turn blender to low speed and gently add 3–4 tablespoons olive oil, drop by drop, and lemon juice and ice water. Without turning blender off, add 1 cup olive oil in a thin stream that breaks into droplets occasionally. From the first drop of olive oil to the last, never stop blending on low speed.

Aioli is delicious served with cold platters of beef and fish with hot boiled potatoes and garnishes of tomatoes, olives, hard-cooked-egg quarters, and the like.

As an appetizer, try it as an enticing garlic dip with raw vegetables. Or spoon it on blanched chilled broccoli flowerets or asparagus spears (see Index) as a dinner vegetable.

SERVES 4 WITH ENTREE, 6–10 WITH APPETIZERS

Note: Always assemble all your mayonnaise ingredients, perfectly measured, before you start the blending process. This is important, because the whole thing takes only a minute or two, and starting and stopping the blender may thin or thicken the sauce improperly. Ingredients should be cool or chilled a bit, never lukewarm.

MAYONNAISE

Freshly made mayonnaise is a rapturously delicious substance. The rapture increases when you realize how quickly it can be made in a blender.

1 large egg

¼ teaspoon dry mustard

½ teaspoon salt

1½ tablespoons lemon juice

1 cup good light olive oil (such as Bertoli)

1 teaspoon ice water, if necessary

Drop the egg, mustard, and salt into blender and whirl at high speed until very thick and foamy, about 45 seconds. Reduce speed to low and add lemon juice. Leaving blender on, start to pour the oil into top of blender in a stream so thin that it breaks into droplets. By the time the oil is all poured in, the mayonnaise will be ready. If it thickens too much for blending to continue, thin by adding the ice water.

SERVES 6–10

GREENERY MAYONNAISE

Green mayonnaise adds verdant glamour to many more dishes besides poached salmon. This pretty variation is made by adding 3–5 tablespoons spinach, parsley, and/or fresh herbs to the mayonnaise. Blanching the greens brightens their green color, and also helps preserve freshness. Green mayonnaise can be refrigerated for a few days, but not so long as regular mayonnaise.

Blanch the vegetables and/or herbs in boiling water for 1 minute, then rinse quickly under cold water and pat dry. Follow mayonnaise recipe above, and add greens to the blender at the end of the whirling process.

TOMATO MAYONNAISE

Use this as a handsome spoon-on or dipping mayonnaise for raw vegetables. Pretty on cold shrimp (cooked), or a salad dish of cucumber, onion, and celery slices with black olives.

> 1 cup mayonnaise
> 1 tomato, chopped
> 4 ounces canned or fresh tomato sauce

Stir together and chill for at least half an hour to blend flavors. Fresh basil may be added as a garnish, or ¼ teaspoon dried basil blended into mayonnaise.

SERVES 4 WITH ENTREES, 6–10 WITH APPETIZERS OR AS DIP

8. DESSERTS

DESSERTS IN THE RAW

A fragrance of fresh fruits. A mélange of sweet spices blending into a honeyed stream. Billows of sweet whipped cream. Fresh milk ripening into tangy fruit-drenched yogurt and kefir and an infinity of cheeses from everywhere on the earth. Toppings and textures, sweetmeated and chewy, of every kind of nut and seed.

All the great cuisines are rich in fresh desserts made of foods meant to be eaten in the raw. Many are time- and palate-honored classics dating back to antiquity. Fruits and honeys and cheeses were popular in Roman times, in Biblical times, as well as in Early American traditional cooking. Today tropical fruits have brought a sweet new excitement to our desserts and refrigerated shipping techniques make it possible to enjoy an astonishing range of fruits, some grown thousands of miles away.

The great stars of the raw-dessert world are fruits. They are delicious raw, eaten out of hand, sliced or mixed, because they are bursting with sweet natural sugars.

They are also irresistibly good with the traditional accompaniments listed below. Browse through the list and then experiment. You can't go wrong, and some of your own casual combinations with local fruits in season will prove incredibly good. The recipes in this section should give you some good ideas.

Creams: Whipped cream, vanilla cream, ice cream, soured cream, clotted cream, thick pours of country cream, all heavenly with any fruit.

Milks, kefir, buttermilk: Fresh, sweet milk, certified raw milk or pasteurized milk, churned buttermilk, and, in some areas, fruited kefir that is a dessert all by itself.

Yogurt: Plain and tangy on fruits, delicious with stirs of honey, fabulous when flavored with fruit or served in fruit sundaes.

Honey: Not just honey, but a swarm of honeys from a thousand regions, nurtured by the blossoms of many different flowers and fruits and wheats, each with its own super-sweet glamour.

Nuts: Sweetmeats, tasting of a hundred subtly different but sensational flavors, each nestled tightly, richly, in its own perfect shell.

Spices: Whispers of nutmeg, the sweet hotness of ginger root, glorious cinnamon, aromatic allspice, all to sprinkle with abandon in a thousand desserts.

Cheeses: Everywhere in the world, wherever cows graze, each country, each county, each region creates its own cheeses. The variations are deliciously endless, the romantic stories of origins often told. With fruit, they become very special desserts.

Wines and liqueurs: The grapes and fruits of summer, fermented and aged into the spirits of fall and winter. Naturally, they have a luscious affinity for the fruits from which they came. They are the source of a thousand dessert triumphs.

FRUITS

Like vintage wines, fruits vary in flavor and sweetness from season to season, and from orchard to orchard. They're beautiful, and inclined to be temperamental. One year they may need sweetening with a little sugar; the next, they will be drenched in natural sweetness all their own. So never judge a fruit by one season, or one variety. Keep experimenting.

SHOPPING FOR FRUITS

Each fruit has its own special personality, and you can't always tell by looking: Those slightly speckled pears may be tender and mouth-watering, the duller apples may be the most delicious, green-tinged oranges may be beautifully ripe. Like a book, you can't tell a fruit by its cover. And outer perfection may not always mean perfect inner flavor.

The best way is to buy just one of a fruit, and *take a bite.* If the bite is so-so, move on. If the bite is sweet and good, stock up—buy as many of that fruit as you can comfortably feast on. In this manner, you will gradually acquire a sharper eye, and become accustomed to the particular fruits of your region. Many fabulous local varieties of fruit simply stay local; they do not ship well.

DISPLAYING FRUITS IN A FRUIT BOWL

The perfect place to keep many fruits at home is in a fruit bowl, in easy reach of everyone, for snacking and breakfasting and impulsive dessert thoughts. Many fruits ripen nicely at room temperature. Only a few, like berries, are so fragile as to need constant refrigeration. A fruit bowl is a lovely thing to have around. It's more beautiful than a bowl of flowers, and doesn't cost a decorating penny.

STORING FRUITS

Once a fruit is very ripe, it should be eaten. If not, keep it in the refrigerator to arrest the ripening process. Some people stash fruit bowls in the refrigerator at night.

Often, the thinner the skin, the more fragile and more speedily ripened (and perishable) the fruit. Hard or tough-skinned fruits (apples, avocados, pineapples, oranges, pomegranates, to name a few) will last much longer at room temperature, and keep much longer in the refrigerator.

CUTTING UP FRUITS

Once you cut up a fruit, the quicker you eat it the better. Fruits are simply brimming with natural sugars in a very juicy form, and their sparkling enzymes and nutrients begin to lose their zest soon after you cut the skin open. (That's why some turn brown if you leave them out, sliced.) Tumble them in lemon juice with a little sugar added, and they'll stay fresh until serving time.

BEAUTIFUL, TIME-SAVING FRUIT SLICERS: TOYS FOR CHILDREN, TOO

Browse through the housewares department at your local store, or in one of the gourmet kitchen shops. You'll find a fetching group of fruit slicers (vegetable slicers, too) that reduce fruit-slicing time to almost zero.

Apple slicers press down and flower-slice an apple in 1 second. Good for pears and tomatoes, too.

Melon ballers can be used on any tender, melonlike fruit, plus bananas, persimmons, papayas, and even jello and ice cream.

Zigzag cutters offer tempting possibilities, along with little star cutters and the like. They all make fast work out of fancy fruit-work.

And children adore them. Every child deserves an apple slicer and a melon baller for fun at breakfast and dessert. What better way to eat a cantaloupe than with your own melon-spoon?

FRUITS: TO PEEL OR NOT TO PEEL?

The lazy way is definitely the more nutritious way. Peels of fruit with thinner edible skins, such as apples, peaches, plums, pears, nectarines, apricots, are more than good to eat—they're good for you. When you peel, you throw away a certain amount of nutrients that lie in and just under the skin. So whenever you can, don't peel. Don't work. Don't lift a finger. Just relax and eat.

THE FRUIT-CHEESE-NUT CENTERPIECE DESSERT

This allows you to create an insanely extravagant centerpiece, throwing money around. Later, you get all your money back, because you eat the centerpiece after dinner.

1 large fruit (cantaloupe, bunch
    bananas, pineapple
    even an eggplant)
different-colored apples
a few other fruits (pears, grapes,
    etc.) for variety

½ pound assorted nuts in the
    shell
assorted cheeses (partially cut by
    you in wedges and/or
    some little individually
    wrapped cheeses)

Use a wooden board or long skinny tray you can set in the middle of your table. (If you have nothing suitable, use two or three layers of plastic wrap or a piece of transparent plastic as center base.) Heap fruits on base, setting in 2 tall, thin, colorful candles with fruit (use a low candlestick, or partially core two apples and stick candles inside). Put highest or large fruits in center and let lower ones spill out at either end. Fill in gaps with nuts, cheese, a few leaves from one of your house plants.

MACÉDOINE DE FRUITS RAFRAÎCHIS
MEDLEY OF FRESH FRUITS

*3 cups fresh fruits, peeled and
  sliced (peaches, nec-
  tarines, cantaloupe, pears,
  apricots, bananas, etc.) or
  whole (raspberries,
  strawberries)*

*½ cup sugar
½ cup water
3 tablespoons cointreau, cassis,
  maraschino, or other
  liqueur (optional)
sprinkling of fresh almonds, split*

Select 2–4 fruits for your macédoine. Make a sugar syrup by boiling sugar and water for 5 minutes, or until syrupy. Pour some over fruit and mix all with liqueur. Cover and chill. Serve, garnished, within a few hours or the fruit flavors will lose their individuality.

SERVES 4–6

QUICK COUPE DE FRUITS RAFRAÎCHIS
If your supply of fresh fruits is limited, try mixing readily available fresh fruit like bananas and pineapple with canned mixed fruits for a casual fall or winter fruit cup. Garnishes of powdered sugar, chocolate bits, or shredded coconut might be used. Or pass a little jug of rum at the table for those who wish to spike as well as spice their fruit.

A CLASSIC MACÉDOINE OF FRUITS

*1 apple
2 pineapple slices
4 figs, quartered
2 peaches*

*2 oranges
2 bananas
lemon juice
sugar*

MIXED LIQUEUR DRESSING
*2 peach stone kernels (nuts concealed
   within seed shell)
6 tablespoons sugar
grated orange and lemon rind*

*1 tablespoon kirsch
1 tablespoon maraschino
1 tablespoon curaçao
1 pear, peeled and mashed*

Peel and slice fruits into separate bowls, so fruit flavors will not blend together; save any juice. Sprinkle fruits with lemon juice and a tiny bit of sugar to prevent darkening. Chill.

Hammer peach stones open to release kernel "nuts," then crush these with sugar and grated rind. Mix with other dressing ingredients and reserved fruit juices.

At serving time, bring bowls of fruit and sauce to table. Toss all together and dish out. Pass a bowl of whipped cream, with a little sugar and vanilla added, if you like.

SERVES 6–8

CREME CHANTILLY WITH FRUITS
(VANILLA-SPIKED WHIPPED CREAM)

Nothing in the whole world is quite as delicious as whipped cream, sweetened with vanilla added, and served on fruit.

Note: Everybody loves whipped cream, but too many call it fattening or too rich. This is just too silly for words. If you're serving whipped cream on *fresh fruits,* you are definitely in low and medium calorie territory if you go a bit light on the cream. Remember, whipping makes cream very light; it expands because it's filled with air. Here's an example. A whole apple, sliced and dipped into sweetened whipped cream, will often be less than 150 calories. One slice of apple pie will cost 350–450 calories!

SUGAR WITH A VANILLA BEAN

For luscious goodies like sugar sprinkled on fruits and sugar sweetened whipped cream, fill a glass jar with sugar and stick a whole dried vanilla bean (in spice department of supermarket) into the middle of the sugar. Seal the jar tightly. Give the vanilla bean a few days to slowly add its heavenly flavor to the sugar, and then use as needed. A vanilla bean is more than gourmet tradition—it is a lovely way to make every teaspoon full of sugar you use taste much more sugary and delicious. No sweet tooth should be without it.

FRUITS SOUTH AMERICANA

*6-ounce can frozen orange juice,
    undiluted*
2 tablespoons tequila

1 box strawberries
1 pineapple, with leaf crown-top on
2 papayas

Thaw orange concentrate until mushy and blend with tequila. Wash and cap strawberries. Add half the orange mixture to strawberries, toss to coat berries, and chill several hours. Cut pineapple into four quarters lengthwise, leaving leaf crown on fruit. Cut meat away from these quarters, then dice meat and toss with remaining orange mixture. Refrigerate several hours.

Just before serving, cut papayas in half. Scoop out seeds and fill papaya halves with strawberry mixture. Arrange pineapple cubes in shells. Arrange papaya halves and pineapple quarters on plate.

SERVES 8

HAWAIIAN FRUIT DIP PLATTER WITH RUM

*1 coconut, broken into dip-size
    pieces*
½ pineapple, cut into chunks
*1 papaya, cut into chunks, speared
    with toothpicks*

1 banana, cut into fat chunks
*1 bowl (16 ounces) sweetened
    whipped cream, spiked
    with rum*

Arrange fruits around bowl of whipped cream on platter or tray. Try this for a spectacular breakfast or brunch, or for a dessert party.

SERVES 6–12

FRUIT KERNEL CENTERS
Fruits with a big seed in the center, such as peaches, nectarines, and apricots, have a tangy little "nut" inside that is fun to eat. Some people like to sprinkle this nut, crushed, on the fruit itself, or mixed in with a topping of brown sugar and crushed almonds. There is even a liqueur made of fruit kernels steeped in spirits: crème de noyaux.

FRUITS WITH LIQUEURS

Many liqueurs are made with fruits, and so, not surprisingly, fruits are very good with a variety of liqueurs. Here are some of the variations you might want to try: Marinate fruits in liqueurs for a few hours; sprinkle on a few drops; mix a few drops in with sweetened whipped cream toppings; pass liqueurs at the table; or serve each cup of fruit with a glass jigger filled with liqueur. Each person pours on his liqueur to taste.

Some of the traditional liqueurs used with fruit desserts include imported cassis, banana liqueur, brandy, calvados, cherry liqueur, cura-çao, Grand Marnier, Kahlua, kirsch, kummel, and, of course, rum, sherry, and wine. And don't forget champagne!

FRUITS OVER . . . OR UNDER . . . ICE CREAM

Fresh fruits are delicious with ice cream. If you soften the ice cream and heap on fruit, it takes the place of a whipped cream. Garnish with shavings of chocolate, or mint leaves dredged in powdered sugar.

Try peach ice cream (with most fruits), vanilla ice cream (with every fruit), fruit ices (with any fruit, plus whipped cream), raspberry ice cream (with peaches), pineapple ice cream (with strawberries), mocha or coffee ice cream (with pineapple), chocolate or fudge ice cream (with bananas).

FRUITS WITH MILK AND SUGAR

Just because this is so easy, so casual, don't forget it's the most luscious breakfast, brunch, lunch, dinner, or midnight dessert you can eat.

FRUITS WITH BROWN SUGAR AND SOUR CREAM

Another great classic, loved and famous in homes and restaurants all over the world.

THE UBIQUITOUS APPLE

With cool aplomb, the apple travels with you—in bag lunches, in cars, in suitcases, to executive meetings, to school, to church (seen more in Europe than here), on camping trips, to movies (good with popcorn, you know). Unperturbed by heat or by cold, its tight skin holds in all that crunchy, sweet moisture. Piled in a fruit bowl, it can be ignored or eaten, as you will. It will look so beautiful you'll want to paint it, as painters have for centuries. Where would the still life be without the apple?

SHOPPING FOR APPLES

Someone is always trying to teach me which apple is which. But I never learn, because there seems to be an endless variety of red, green, and yellow apples. You don't have to be an expert. All you have to do is decide if the apple tastes good to you.

WHICH ARE THE BEST APPLES?

If there are four bins of different apples, buy one of each kind and take a bite. Use this method on all biteable fruits.

THE APPLE AS HEALTH SNACK

If you have a sweet tooth, the apple will not decay it, as many snacks will; like all fresh fruits, its sugar is natural sugar. Even better, eating an apple with its skin on is like brushing your teeth, too. It cleans teeth and gums. Don't bother peeling apples, because the skin has Vitamin C hiding right inside it. And apples—especially the skin—abound with tasty nutrients.

As for constipation, it's unknown when there are things like apples around. The apple, like many fruits, has distinct digestive advantages.

So bye, bye Miss American pie. Eat the apple that inspired the pie instead.

INSTANT APPLE PIE À LA MODE

1½ cups vanilla ice cream left out to soften
4 apples, cored
1 cup sweet granola mixed with graham cracker crumbs (or crushed
     sugar cookies)

Leave ice cream out to soften. When it is soft enough to be stirred, slice apples into 4 individual dishes on top of a layer of granola/graham crackers or sugar cookies. Pour ice cream over apples and granola and serve at once.

SERVES 4

APPLE SLICES WITH WHIPPED CREAM DIP

heavy cream, whipped and sweetened with sugar and vanilla
3 large apples, sliced

Put whipped cream in dip bowl in center of platter. Arrange apple slices in circle around dip, and pass.

SERVES 4–6

GREAT CHEESES TO SERVE WITH APPLES
Brie	*Gruyère*
Edam	*Stilton*
Gouda	*And, of course, the classic cheddars*
Gourmandaise	

APRICOTS

Alas, the season is all too short for this creamily delicious fruit. Apricot trees are sensitive to weather, so when it's a good year for apricots, serve them lavishly at every meal. Put them out in candy bowls mixed with big cherries for desserts or snacks. Serve them instead of a dinner vegetable with pork, ham, or chicken. Serve sliced apricots with whipped cream. Drizzle diced apricots with apricot brandy and a sprinkling of powdered sugar.

APRICOT MOUSSE

5 apricots, fresh (or 12 dried)
½ cup cream whipped stiffly, with 1 teaspoon vanilla added
3–4 tablespoons powdered sugar (depending on tartness of fruit)
⅓ cup sliced or crushed almonds

Remove apricot pits. Dice apricots, leaving skins on. and whirl in blender with just enough whipped cream (about 3 tablespoons) to permit easy blending. Fold blended apricot mixture and sugar into remaining whipped cream. Serve in sherbet or champagne glasses with nuts sprinkled generously on top.

SERVES 4

Note: If dried apricots are used, soak them in water overnight to soften.

BANANAS IN THE RAW

This marvelous fruit needs little introduction. As the song says, you should not store bananas in the refrigerator, but do chill them briefly if you're in the mood. Bananas must be sliced just before serving, or tumbled in a little citrus juice to keep them from turning dark. Buy them green and they'll turn yellow in your fruit bowl. When the yellow skin gets brown speckles, they're good and ripe. Only when they turn brown *inside* are they overripe.

WHY BANANAS ARE WORTH GOING BANANAS OVER

If you like bananas, there is absolutely no reason why you shouldn't make a monkey out of yourself and eat them once a day. They happen to be so digestible you can hand one (peeled) to your six-month-old as soon as he sprouts a tooth—and serve them mashed to littler babies. And they're loaded with a truly outstanding array of nutrients, including potassium and lots of vitamins. They even boast some protein. Calorie-wise, they are a wise choice.

BANANA POTPOURRI WITH BRANDY OR RUM SAUCE

A Scandinavian import, this sweet sauce, called Eggedosis, is spiked with fragrant rum or brandy. It works compatibly with the tartness of fresh fruits, as well as the smooth flavor of bananas.

1 large chopped banana (or 2 small)

1 cup halved seedless grapes

1 apple, chopped and peeled

1 small orange, peeled, sectioned, and chopped

¾ cup pecans and/or walnuts, chopped

EGGEDOSIS SAUCE

2 egg whites
5 egg yolks
5 tablespoons sugar
1–2 tablespoons brandy or rum

Toss the fruits in the sauce and chill before serving. The sauce should taste heady, but very sweet. Add more sugar if necessary.

SERVES 4

GRANDPA'S BANANA-HONEY SHAKE

Sweet and serene in flavor, with a hidden tang. Children respond to this shake, because it has banana, honey, and milk, all beloved foods. In the summer it's cool and refreshing, supplying easy energy. In the winter, when you have a scratchy throat, it makes a soothing cough syrup.

1 pint milk

1 tablespoon or more honey

1 banana

¼–⅓ cup pineapple juice

1 dash lemon juice (3 drops or so)

Blend until foamy, adding lemon juice just a second before you turn off blender. Add an egg and it's a meal. Taste. If too rich, add more milk.

SERVES 1–2

BERRIES IN THE RAW

Some fruits, like berries, have everything. They're rich, gorgeous to look at, prepared by nature in ready-to-eat shapes, easy to fix, and delicious. They're even low-calorie, if you're interested.

Each berry, in each region of our country, has its own local color and special flavor. Their names are a delectable litany: blackberries, strawberries, raspberries, blueberries, huckleberries, loganberries, boysenberries, lingonberries, and more. Go exploring at the market, and out in the country. No childhood is complete without berry-picking, as berries are delicious off-the-vine fresh. Just be sure the berries are familiar to you.

Eat berries quickly. They overripen easily and should be refrigerated. Their seasons are short, so hurry.

BERRIES WITH WHIPPED CREAM AND SOUR CREAM

All berries are fabulous with whipped and sour cream. Taste berries and add sugar only if too tart. Brown sugar is good with sour cream.

BREAKFAST BERRIES

With milk and sugar, a glorious way to start the day.

INSTANT FRESH BERRY PIE

2 cups crushed lemon cookies or
    wafers
1/4 cup softened butter
2–4 cups fresh blueberries, raspberries, strawberries, blackberries, or a mix of these berries

1/8 cup or more sugar
1 1/2 cups whipped heavy cream
1/8 cup grated sweetened coconut
    (optional)

Mix cookies and butter together and press into a pie pan, making a thick layer. Put in freezer to firm. Tumble berries in the sugar, slicing enough berries so that berry juice mixes in with sugar. Taste and add more sugar if needed. Just before serving, pack berries into pie shell. Swirl whipped cream prettily on top and sprinkle with coconut.

SERVES 6

Variations: Tumble the berries in crème de cassis, or another dessert liqueur you're fond of. Use less sugar.

For a tutti-frutti pie, combine berries with other fruits, or use fresh fruits at hand, such as peaches or plums. Relatively soft fruits are best and they should be peeled.

LEN'S LOW-CALORIE BLUEBERRY FLIP

⅓ cup skim-milk powder
shaved ice (a few ice cubes, smashed in a towel)
1 box fresh or frozen blueberries
1 teaspoon low-calorie sweetener to taste

Blend in blender. Serve at once, heaped in sherbet cups. Garnish with a few fresh blueberries, dusted with powdered sugar.

SERVES 4

RASPBERRIES

Their natural season is July, and for a few precious weeks you should lose your head and your heart to raspberries. You can have hothouse raspberries during other times of the year, but they are tagged with prices almost as elegant as the raspberry.

Each berry is a delicate dynamo of subtle delight, light, but so gently sweet, so luxurious, it virtually melts in your mouth. Fresh raspberries are a dessert in themselves. All you do is nibble one after another, until you subside into pampered satiety.

COOLED RASPBERRIES

Chill and remove a half-hour before serving. Serve them in an iced bowl (a silver bowl looks gorgeous), drenched in cold milk or cream and sprinkled with a little sugar.

SCANDINAVIAN RED-FRUIT PUDDING

The classic Rodgrod Med Flod. Some say it was the inspiration for Jello, but in my view any resemblance to Jello deserves a Bronx raspberry.

¾ *pound fresh raspberries* (*or 1 10-ounce package frozen raspberries, thawed*)	½ *cup water*
	3 tablespoons sugar
	½ *pint heavy cream*
1 packet or less Knox gelatin	*powdered sugar*
¼ *cup warm water*	

Wash berries and whirl at high speed in blender till puréed. Melt gelatin in warm water and heat, stirring just till dissolved. Add gelatin mixture, water, and sugar to raspberries in blender and whirl for 1–2 minutes at high speed. Taste and add more sugar or a pinch of salt if you like, or perhaps a little more water. Purée should be sweet but tart, to contrast with bland cream topping.

Now quickly (it jells soon) pour into individual dessert cups (or a fancy mold, if you want to unmold and serve a creation). Whip heavy cream to soft, not stiff, consistency, adding a bit of sugar and vanilla. Serve each bowl topped with a sprinkling of powdered sugar and the soft-whipped cream.

The tangy raspberry flavor, played against the soft cream, makes this a delectably rich dessert . . . so plan on small helpings.

SERVES 6–8

RASPBERRIES WITH SOFTENED VANILLA ICE CREAM
A simple, but endearing combination.

RASPBERRY FOOL

Fools date back to heaven knows when. They are simple but plush, and can be made with quite a few fruits. The addition of cassis makes it all rather sophisticated, and so delicious. When they wrote "Fools rush in . . . where angels fear to tread . . ." maybe they were inspired by a cool raspberry fool.

2 cups puréed raspberries, sweetened to taste
1 tablespoon cassis or rum
1 cup cream, whipped

Fold fruit and cassis into whipped cream. Chill well in pretty serving bowl or in individual dishes. Garnish with mint dipped in powdered sugar or a single raspberry.

SERVES 4–6

STRAWBERRIES

Fresh-strawberry season comes but once a year (unless you pay premium prices), so when you see those pretty boxes, indulge yourself.

GIANT STRAWBERRIES DIPPED IN POWDERED SUGAR
An opulent yet simple dessert.

WHOLE STRAWBERRIES AND WHIPPED CREAM
Unspeakably good. Add sugar only if berries are tart.

STRAWBERRIES AU IRISH WHISKEY

Irish coffee is not the only way to go.

1 pound strawberries
¾ pint coffee ice cream
6 tablespoons Irish whiskey
½ pint sweetened whipped cream

Wash and hull the strawberries and pile in cocktail glasses over coffee ice cream. Top with spoonfuls of whipped cream with Irish whiskey drizzled on top.

SERVES 6

STRAWBERRIES AND COINTREAU

These two have been having an affair since cointreau was created.

1 pound strawberries
4 tablespoons cointreau

Wash and halve the strawberries to bring out flavor. Tumble in cointreau and refrigerate for 1–3 hours. Remove 15 minutes before serving. If not sweet enough, sprinkle on a bit of powdered sugar just as you bring to the table.

SERVES 6

BING CHERRIES

Bing cherries, and other sweet cherries, are perfect eaten in the raw. They are beautiful just as they are. No work, just instant elegance.

BING CHERRIES IN SOUR CREAM

1 pound Bing cherries, stems on if possible
4 ounces sour cream

Cluster the cherries around a bowl of icy-cold sour cream. Each person dips cherries into sour cream. The cherries are good chilled, served at room temperature, or even warmed a bit in the sun—delicious any way you dip them.

SERVES 4

BING CHERRIES DIPPED IN GRAND MARNIER

Cherries are classically good with spirits. This recipe combines the after-dinner liqueur with dessert in an amiable way.

10 ounces Grand Marnier, poured into 6 small liqueur glasses
1½ pounds Bing cherries (or other sweet cherries)

Put the liqueur glasses of Grand Marnier on 6 small dessert plates, each with a generous handful of cherries. Each person dips the cherries, one by one, into the liqueur. If there is any liqueur left, simply sip it. Other fruity liqueurs can be substituted for the Grand Marnier.

SERVES 6

COCONUT

This huge, one-seeded fruit grows on a variety of coconut palms in the tropics. We use it lavishly with fruits, and in coconut cakes, sometimes forgetting that coconut meat itself is an entrancingly chewy delight.

Nowadays, coconuts are available at most markets everywhere. All you have to do is shake the coconut—if you hear the sound of coconut liquid sloshing around inside, the coconut is nice and fresh.

OPENING THE COCONUT

If you approach a coconut with enthusiasm but ignorance, you are liable to have a few problems. Seized by a primeval tropical urge, I made my first attempt with other members of my eighth-grade class after school one day. We used a hammer, almost perished laughing while we attacked the stubborn shell, and ultimately managed to break it open, but it was so mangled, so crushed, that we barely ate a single bite. We also made a big mess in the kitchen.

Actually, cracking a coconut is ridiculously simple. The hard outer shell of the coconut has 3 brown indentations, called "eyes," at one end of the shell. All you do is:

1. Pierce the eyes by hammering in an ice pick or a big nail, 1″ or so deep. If you can't find the eye, just pierce a hole anywhere.

2. Upend the pierced coconut on a bowl, letting the coconut juice drain out. This juice is good to drink. The coconut will now be very easy to open, because there is air space inside it.

3. Hammer, gently tapping in a circle around the shell. It will break apart easily. Break apart the great big pieces of coconut into somewhat smaller 2″ or 3″ pieces by laying them down, rounded side up, and tapping again with the hammer.

4. Some of the coconut meat breaks away from the shell naturally. The rest you gently pry away with a nutpick or the tip of a small knife.

The chunks of coconut meat you have removed from the coconut shell are ready to eat. They have a very thin brown skin that can be cut away for grating, if you wish. However, this thin skin is good, nutritious, pretty, and meant to be eaten. The coconut chunks keep beautifully for several days in the refrigerator.

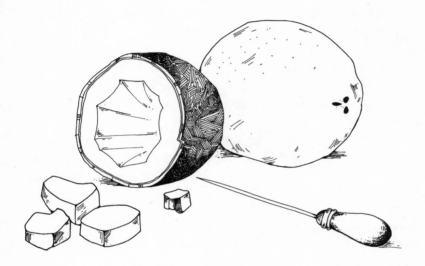

COCONUT WITH RUM/HONEY DIP

Half the fun of this dish is the primitive look of the broken chunks of gleaming white coconut.

1 coconut
¼ cup honey
¼ cup rum, or to taste

Open and prepare coconut as noted above. Chill. Mix honey and rum in a small glass. Arrange coconut in bite-size pieces (¾"–1½") on tray, lined with leaves or ferns or even a leafy pineapple top. (For parties, add pineapple chunks speared with toothpicks.) If you have individual wooden serving planks, coconut can be served on these with a shot glass of rum-honey mixture on each.

BROWN-SUGARED FRESH COCONUT

As an introduction to raw coconut, many people like it—especially children, and be sure to remind them to chew it well—with just the tiniest sprinkle of brown sugar because they can see the sugar bits. As you become used to eating coconut, you'll find it tastes naturally sweet without sugar.

GRATED FRESH COCONUT

If you are grating your own, the proper way is to remove the brown skin with a paring knife and grate it against a grater, doing one piece at a time. A faster, if not quite so perfect way, is to grate it in the blender with water, then quickly pour off the water. Coconut does not chop up in the blender as easily as nuts do. Grated fresh coconut—sweetened or unsweetened—can also be purchased in many markets and health food stores.

Something wonderful happens when you mix grated coconut with fresh fruits. The myriad fruit and coconut mixtures are properly called ambrosia. They are all heavenly, truly the food of the gods, and you can create your own with whatever fruits you have at hand in your area.

Basically, sliced fruits are arranged in layers in a glass bowl, with each layer sprinkled liberally with grated coconut (and a bit of sugar if the coconut is unsweetened or the fruit is very tart). Then you pour over all a bit of orange juice, sherry, cointreau, kirsch, or white wine and let it chill briefly in the refrigerator. Served in a glass bowl, it is very colorful.

HAWAIIAN AMBROSIA

2 cups pineapple cubes
1 cup diced papaya (optional)
½ cup maraschino cherries
8–10 marshmallows, quartered
    (definitely optional)

1 large banana, sliced
¾–1 cup fresh grated coconut

Combine pineapple, papaya, cherries, and marshmallows. Chill. Just before serving, add banana and coconut. Toss lightly and bring to the table heaped in two pineapple half-shells. Or serve in sherbet glasses. Fruits can be varied—for example, substitute cut-up orange or pear for papaya, or add apple bits (at the last, since they, like bananas, turn brown unless dipped in citrus juice). If you have them, add sprigs of mint leaves dipped in powdered sugar.

SERVES 6

CRANBERRIES

CRANBERRIES OVER ICE CREAM
Cranberries are too tart to eat raw, but when that tartness is combined with something sweet, the flavor of cranberries becomes a passion. And they're loaded with Vitamin C. Try them crushed in the blender with sugar and a little water. Add a little sweet liqueur to this instant syrup and spoon over vanilla ice cream.

FRESH CRANBERRY JELLO

1½ cups water
¾ cup cranberries
⅓ cup sugar
1 package lemon Jello

½ orange
¼–½ cup nutmeats
whipped cream

Blend ½ cup of the water and cranberries in blender. Add sugar and let stand until sugar dissolves. Dissolve Jello in remaining water. Add orange to blender and blend. Pour into Jello mixture, add nutmeats, and chill in mold. Top with whipped cream.

SERVES 4

KIWIFRUIT

Now is the time to create divine desserts with this bizarre and soon-to-be-bountiful fruit. Once an exotic import from China, or more frequently New Zealand, the kiwifruit is now being grown with conspicuous success in a number of areas in the United States.

The kiwifruit proves that beauty is more than skin deep. For beneath its brown, fuzzy, and rather boring outside skin dwells brilliant emerald-green flesh, blazing with a fresh, cool beauty. Each slice is a pretty design in itself, centered with tiny edible seeds. All you have to do with the kiwi is peel the soft skin and simply slice it. Whole, it keeps quite obligingly in the refrigerator for at least a week after you bring it home. Kiwifruit tastes like an especially delicious strawberry, with a little extra tang that is definitely kiwi. And once you've tasted its sweet flavor, you'll find it a favorite for fruit desserts.

KIWIFRUIT IN THE RAW

3 kiwifruit

Peel and slice the kiwifruit and arrange on a pretty platter. If kiwifruit is new to you, you may wish to add other sliced fruits to the platter, with the brilliant green of the kiwi a happy new accent.

SERVES 4

KIWIFRUIT SHORTCAKE WITH
POMEGRANATE SEEDS

4 kiwifruit
6 slices of poundcake (or shortcake)
1 4-ounce container of heavy cream, whipped
½ pomegranate, or about 5 tablespoons pomegranate seeds

Peel and slice the kiwifruit, reserving 6 slices or tiny wedges for decorating. Assemble like a shortcake, just before serving, with 1 slice of
poundcake topped by sliced fruit, topped by whipped cream. Scatter
pomegranate seeds over whipped cream, and a slice of kiwifruit.

SERVES 6

LIMES

FROSTED LIME PIE

This is a gossamer concoction that dependably turns out light and
fluffy. The tangy, icy-sweet lime filling is just as featherlight as the
whipped cream topping. The pie is frozen without the topping and
awaits your bidding. Whip it out 10 minutes before serving and slather
on the whipped cream.

GRAHAM CRACKER CRUST
1¼ cups graham cracker crumbs
¼ cup superfine sugar
¼ cup butter, at room temperature

Mix together and press into pie plate.

FILLING
5 eggs, separated
¾ cup superfine sugar, or more if
    limes are very tart
⅔ cup fresh squeezed, strained
    lime juice

2 teaspoons finely grated lime rind
⅛ teaspoon salt
3 teaspoons gelatin powder

TOPPING

1½ cups heavy cream, whipped
thin slices lime or a few fresh strawberries
sugar

Sweeten whipped cream with 1 teaspoon sugar, or more to taste. Mix crust ingredients and press into pie plate. Separate eggs. Beat yolks in top of double boiler over steaming, not boiling, water. (If yolks start to coagulate, take off heat.) When yolks have thickened, continue beating, adding ½ cup of the sugar gradually until all is pale and thick. Add lime juice and grated rind, stirring until mixture coats back of spoon. Remove from heat. While yolk mixture is cooling, beat the egg whites with the salt until soft peaks form. Gradually beat in the remaining sugar until stiff and shiny. Just before you combine the yolk mixture and whites, dissolve the gelatin powder in a tiny amount of water over a flame. Add a little of the yolk to gelatin and water. Stir dissolved gelatin into the yolk mixture, with ⅓ fluffy egg whites. Then fold in remaining meringue mixture until evenly distributed. Taste, and add a speck of sugar if lime flavor is very tart. Turn into pie shell and pop into freezer.

At serving time, remove 10 minutes before final presentation. Cover with the whipped cream, swirled about generously. Garnish with a slice of lime or two, or a few fresh strawberries. Filling will be icy-cold and magnificently light.

SERVES 6–8

Note: If you have extra filling that you can't fit in the pie shell, put it in custard cups and put them in the freezer for another sweet occasion. It freezes well.

MANGOES

There is a mango display at the local market, and a great, big, tough-looking guy strolls up to it. He looks at the mangoes and picks out one, two, three, four, and puts them in his shopping cart. Curiosity gets the better of my manners.

"You must really like mangoes," I say. "Did you learn to eat them in Hawaii?"

"Oh, no."

"Well, how did you get so involved with mangoes?"

"Oh." He smiles. "On Truk."

"Truk?"

"Truk, the island in the Pacific. I was there during World War Two, with the Marines. And I've been crazy about mangoes ever since."

He said that one afternoon they stumbled into a native village from the jungle, half dead with heat and exhaustion. A woman brought him a mango and showed him how to slit it open like a banana with his pocketknife. He said it was the most refreshing, sweetest, most heavenly thing he had ever tasted, and when he was hot and dry and scared and tired, it brought him back to humanity.

HOW A MANGO TASTES
The mango is a peach of a fruit. Golden and juicy, it is indeed reminiscent of the peach. Even better! say the mango-lovers. Indeed, you can treat it as a peach in most recipes, or enjoy it plain. No culinary wizardry is necessary. Like the papaya, the mango is part of a tropical eat wave that's happening at more and more markets.

SELECTING MANGOES
It takes two to mango at the market, for unless you've become a mango buff in Hawaii or South America (or even Truk or New Guinea in the '40s), you'll need some help at first. So ask the man at the produce counter how to pick a good mango, and when is the best time to buy from him.

The mango is a large oval fruit, often rainbow-hued, with a big, flattish pit inside. Pick your mango as you would an avocado. A hard mango is not ripe yet; let it ripen in a fruit bowl. A very soft, mushy mango is too ripe. A firm but yielding dead-weight mango is just right. Eat it right away or keep it in the refrigerator.

HOW TO PEEL AND PIT MANGOES
A mango is large, round, and rather flat. Inside is a large equally flat pit. To remove it, run a knife around the perimeter "edge" of the mango all the way to the pit, holding the mango the flattish way and

cutting through to the edge of the pit. Now take a large kitchen spoon and, starting at one end, carefully push the spoon's curve around the large pit, nudging the flesh up and away from the pit. Turn mango over and repeat on other half of pit. Peel off the skin before or after you pit the mango. Discard the pit and skin, always. They are not edible.

You can also just peel the mango and slice it away from the pit, but you won't end up with decorative slices.

Sliced Mangoes Alone or with Peaches and Whipped Cream

Slice it with peaches or other summer fruits in a macédoine or ambrosia. Serve it with sweetened whipped cream with vanilla added to spoon on top.

The Tropical Mango Popsicle

In South America, it is elegant to serve a whole mango to each person with a sharp knife and fork, on a dessert plate. The mango is picked up and speared at the narrow base with the fork, then held like an ice cream pop. The skin is slit with the knife down from the top, then peeled off like a banana. You eat it like a pop, eating around the pit. (Don't try this at a formal dinner party!)

Mangoes au Granola

An instant but not ordinary meal. Slice mangoes and serve in bowls with granola sprinkled on top. Top that with yogurt or whipped cream, and drizzle honey over all (or sprinkle with brown sugar). Do the same thing with ice cream and call it a mango split, sprinkling nuts on top.

MANGOES AND CHAMPAGNE

Frankly romantic. A little ostentatious, but why not?

To serve before dinner, put a few mango slices in champagne glasses and pour on champagne.

To serve after dinner, assemble:

> *2 mangoes, pitted, peeled, and sliced*
> *1 bottle champagne*
> *2 tablespoons or less sugar*

Tumble mango slices in sugar, fill champagne glasses with slices, and serve. Pour champagne at the table, so everyone can see the spirited display of bubbles. Guests spoon out mangoes, then sip champagne.

SERVES 4–6

THE MELON FAMILY

Each region has its own tempting varieties of melon, and you should experiment with all of them. Casaba, Persian, honeydew, cantaloupe, watermelon, and winter melon are a few of the fabled names. Assorted, they form pale rainbows of sun-washed pastels. And most melon recipes are interchangeable.

CANTALOUPE

This tender, perfect melon, when just ripe, is one of the most popular fruits of all. It needs literally no preparation and is absurdly simple to cut and serve.

There are several schools of thought about selecting a cantaloupe. This method works well for me.

1. Look at it. The webbing of a fine cantaloupe should be thick and raised and very crisscrossy.

2. Touch it. A ripe cantaloupe will be slightly soft at the stem end. If it is quite soft at the stem end, then it is overripe. If there are soft spots on the cantaloupe, it is too ripe.

3. Smell it. The stem end of a ripe cantaloupe should have a cantaloupe fragrance.

THE CANTALOUPE SEASON

Depending on weather variations, you can start looking with eagerness toward late August and September for great bins of big cantaloupes at unbelievably inviting prices. Suddenly the price drops by one-half, or even two-thirds. This is the time to indulge in cantaloupe extravaganzas.

FREEZING CANTALOUPE

One simple way to keep cantaloupes is to peel and slice the cantaloupe and put in freezer containers in orange juice to cover.

CANTALOUPE FOR CHILDREN

Nothing could be easier or more nutritious to serve to children. Even the finicky are tempted by cantaloupe served in halves or thirds, with a melon-baller spoon for each child (or they take turns). These spoons are great fun for children to use, and they will eat almost anything they can use one on.

CANTALOUPE WITH SALT OR LIME

Unnecessary, but some people do enjoy it. If the particular cantaloupe is lacking in full flavor, using salt and/or lime to bring out the flavor.

PICNIC CANTALOUPE

Cut in half and scoop out seeds. Place lime slices in center, put halves back together again, and secure with rubber bands for portability in picnic basket or bag.

CANTALOUPE ICE CREAM RINGS

2 cantaloupes
1 pint vanilla ice cream

Slice cantaloupes (this dish is good with Persian or honeydew melon, too) crosswise into 3 or 4 rings. Cut away skin and seeds. Place one ring on each plate and fill center with scoop of vanilla ice cream. Sprinkle with chocolate shavings or granola if you wish. (Try this sometime with lemon sherbet, watermelon sherbet, pistachio ice cream, or a favorite pudding in the melon rings.)

SERVES 3–4

VEIDA'S
CANTALOUPE CENTERS FRAPPE

Scooped-out seed centers of cantaloupe are usually thrown away. Try saving them and making this delicious, very nutritious frappé drink.

1 cantaloupe center (seeds plus pulp)
1 teaspoon lime juice
½ teaspoon vanilla extract

Blend cantaloupe centers in blender with a *little* water. Sieve out seeds. Stir in lime juice and vanilla to taste. Add a little salt or sugar, depending on your own taste preferences.

SERVES 1–2

A MÉLANGE OF MELON BALLS IN
CANTALOUPE BASKETS

4 cups cantaloupe balls (from about 6 canteloupes)
1 cup watermelon balls (from ¼ watermelon)
1 cup blueberries (optional)
some cointreau
1 pint vanilla ice cream, softened

Marinate fruits in cointreau for at least an hour. Make cantaloupe baskets by cutting down halfway into each cantaloupe from the top, in two cuts about ¾"–1" apart. This forms cantaloupe "handle." Then cut in from either side at halfway mark to meet handle cut (take care not to cut through handle). Pull away the cantaloupe pieces on either side of handle to form baskets. Spoon out seeds, scoop out melon balls, then hollow out basket-shells neatly. Chill baskets. Fill with fruits and pass a bowl of softened vanilla ice cream for topping.

SERVES 6

MELON SLICES VARIÉ

1 casaba melon and/or
1 Persian melon
1 quarter watermelon

1 honeydew melon
1 cantaloupe

Slice each melon open and spoon out seeds. Cut in slender wedges and fan out in an assortment on a big platter.

SERVES 10

WATERMELON

WATERMELON PUNCH BOWL

If you don't have a punch bowl, or even if you do, you should serve watermelon punch in a watermelon punch bowl once every summer. It's a smash at a party.

1 whole watermelon, with
     attractive green skin, not
     too scratched or scarred
1 can apricot juice
1–2 cups orange juice
juice of ½–1 lemon

sprinkling of sugar or honey to
     taste
1–2 cups light rum or vodka or
     gin (optional)
½–1 cup club soda (optional)

Chill the watermelon first. Slice a long, narrow top off the watermelon across the long way, leaving a big enough "brim" for easy ladling. If watermelon doesn't sit firmly, cut a flat sliver off the bottom of melon (before you cut the top), so it won't wobble.

Scoop out watermelon with a spoon and a rounded knife. Seed and chunk the watermelon and put it in the blender. (It will take more than one blenderful to juice the melon.) Now add the juices and the honey and stir well. Taste and add more honey or more tart lemon to adjust punch flavor if punch is to be served without alcohol. Otherwise, pour in the rum and then adjust flavor. You can add some chilled club soda to this or not. Now pour this mixture into the watermelon bowl. Serve very cold, with ice cubes added, set out on a platter and surrounded with green leaves (just pick some from an unsprayed tree or bush), and flowers if you have any handy. Float a few thin lemon slices and perhaps a few berries on top, or just a sprig of mint.

SERVES 6–8

TOSSED WATERMELON BALLS

Cut watermelon in big slices, remove seeds, and cut out as many balls as you can with a melon-ball cutter. Serve heaped in a bowl for dessert, and at the table pour on a dressing of either orange juice or cointreau or rum. (Try a taste of whatever you've got around. Many liqueurs go well with watermelon.) Toss, as though it were a salad, and spoon into dishes.

ORANGES

This awesomely popular fruit is a victim of its own renown. We have used the flavor of orange in so many treats that sometimes, among the many-splendored arrays of "orange" offered to us, we forget the real thing.

A good, sweet, ripe orange is one of the most fragrant, sensual experiences that happens to the human palate. Peel one and see. Taste and smell the orange-blossom fragrance.

ORANGES A LA THE MADRID RITZ

At the Ritz in Madrid, as well as in many other luxury hotels and restaurants in Europe, discriminating diners and their fervent allies, discriminating waiters, appreciate the pristine perfection of a simple ripe orange. An orange for dessert is a ritual, rather than a fussy recipe.

1 sweet orange of high quality per person

A skilled headwaiter, like a talented surgeon, moves with gentle grace. Before you realize what is happening, he peels the orange in one continuous ribbon, starting at the top and finishing at the bottom. The peel falls away in a single spiral. Then he deftly cuts each section from the membranes that define it. Or he simply slices the orange, with lightning speed, into very thin rounds which he arcs gracefully on the plate. Try it. With practice and a very sharp paring knife, you can dazzle your guests.

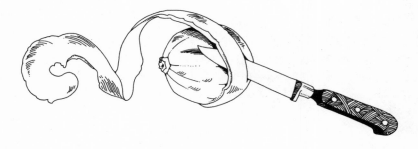

SHERRIED ORANGE AMBROSIA

A magnificent winter dessert that also is served as a cooler all summer. Make in a glass bowl so you can see how lovely it is.

8 sweet oranges
sugar
1½–2 cups grated fresh coconut
sliced bananas and whole strawberries (optional)

½–¾ cup good sherry
fresh mint leaves (optional)

Peel the oranges the easy way with a very sharp small paring knife. Hold over a bowl so juices will be saved. Then slice oranges thinly across into wagon-wheel-looking slices. In a glass bowl, arrange slices in alternating layers with the coconut (and optional fruit, if added). Sprinkle each layer with sugar if desired. Finish with a layer of coconut. Pour reserved orange juice and sherry over all. Cover tightly and chill for at least an hour. Serve with mint leaves.

SERVES 6

After a hot, spicy dinner, the coolness of this dessert is truly ambrosial. For your nectar, you might follow with a touch of brandy and coffee— or Grand Marnier, to preserve the orange-tinted mood.

PAPAYAS IN THE RAW

> The natives here are very strong and live largely on a tree melon called "the fruit of angels."
>
> —CHRISTOPHER COLUMBUS

While you are reaching for a breakfast orange, everyone in tropical countries is reaching for a breakfast papaya. Many a vacationer to tropical isles has brought back a happy addiction to the papaya, and as a result they're now grown here as well as shipped in.

And if the papaya image of lazy tropical days and sumptuous, sensual dining hasn't yet turned you on to papaya, its nutrition will. The papaya has more Vitamin C than oranges, and bewitching special enzymes that do marvelous things for you. Papain, the enzyme found in the papaya tree as well as the fruit, is legendary for its digestive benefits. It's hard to believe that something so sweet and pleasurable could be so good for you, but it's true.

PAPAYA FOR BABIES

Like the banana, the tender papaya, cut into little baby-sized chunks, is a wonderful way to bite into the big world of food.

PAPAYA-ORANGE WHIP—A GOOD INTRODUCTION

Peel and slice up orange and papaya, toss together, and chill. Add banana just before serving. Top with whipped cream sweetened with sugar and a dash of vanilla.

PAPAYA SEEDS

They don't taste as good as the papaya, but some people swear by them. It is said you should only eat six or so at a time, and, like all seed foods, they should be chewed well. They taste tangy, a little like capers. Good in salads.

PAPAYA SLICES WITH DINNER

Sliced papaya is most attractive with grilled meats and ground meats, and good with curries. Think of it as an extra vegetable, or replacing a second vegetable. Or serve it in the dinners where you might have served a warmed peach half (but don't warm it, serve it cool).

PAPAYA-BANANA-HONEY SHAKE

This makes close to a complete breakfast or lunch, as well as a rich dessert, with a vanillalike flavor.

1 small or medium papaya, peeled, seeded, and sliced	*1 tablespoon honey*
	3 eggs
1 big banana, broken	*dash vanilla*
1 squeeze lime (optional but recommended)	*8 ounces milk*

Whirl all ingredients in blender. Taste for sweetness. If it's too thick, add more milk.

SERVES 2–3

This is a great drink for children who tend to loiter over their food until you almost go mad. They slurp these shakes down happily, never dreaming they're filled with so many nourishing goodies.

PEACHES

The peach is one of our most sensual, beautiful fruits, blushing and soft outside, tender and delicately pale-peachy inside, with touches of deep red where the inside of each slice meets the peach pit. Peaches are juicy, so serve them with pretty napkins.

PRETTY PEACH SLICES
After you peel a peach, slice it from top to base in continuous slices. The slices will cling to the pit, so you can cut even slices all the way around. Then press at the top, as though you were breaking an egg, and break the slices away, all at once. They will be nice and even, very pretty to arrange for desserts. Serve with whipped cream (the famed "peaches and cream" of clichédom) or just sprinkled with powdered sugar.

Sliced peaches must be brushed with lemon juice if you're leaving them in refrigerator, or they will change color.

PEACH PIT KERNELS
Hammer open the peach pit and you'll find an oddly appealing tangy little "nut" inside. Eat one plain or with a bit of sugar. Fun.

COLD PEACH DESSERT SOUP WITH FRESH BERRIES

Serve this beautiful "soup" for an unusual dessert, or as first course at a dinner.

1½ cups water
4 cloves
3 tablespoons or more sugar
1 cinnamon stick, broken into pieces
2 tablespoons cornstarch, mixed with ¼ cup water

1 cup dry white wine
3 pounds ripe peaches
1 cup fresh blueberries
1 cup heavy cream

Pour water in saucepan with cloves, sugar, and cinnamon. Bring to a boil, then simmer for 10 minutes. Add cornstarch paste, whipping it into syrup with a wire whisk. Bring to a boil again. Take off stove, stir in the wine, and refrigerate.

Wash peaches, split, and take out pits. Slice enough of the nicest peaches to make about 2 cups and add to the syrup. Cut up the rest and purée in the blender. Then add purée to the syrup mixture. Chill overnight, or at least several hours before serving.

Serve in chilled soup bowls, sprinkled with blueberries. Top with dollop of whipped cream.

SERVES 6–8

PEACH SHAKES

2 large ripe or overripe peaches, peeled   a dash of vanilla
*   and sliced, seed removed   1 or 2 eggs (optional)*
1 pint milk
1 teaspoon honey or 1 tablespoon brown
*   sugar*

Put all in blender and blend until smooth. Taste and add a little more sugar or milk if you wish.

SERVES 2–3

PEACH PIE
Make instant Fresh Fruit Pie. (See Index.) Tumble sliced peaches in a little sugar with cinnamon added.

OVER-RIPE PEACH ICE CREAM

Every once in a while, usually at the height of the midsummer peach season, you discover that those peaches heaped in your fruit bowl are overripe. Or perhaps the market is selling off too-ripe peaches for a handful of pennies. This is the moment you've been waiting for.

2 pounds overripe peaches, peeled   1 cup sweetened condensed milk
and seeded   ½ cup milk
1½ teaspoons lemon juice   1 pint heavy cream, whipped
1½ teaspoons vanilla

Blend milks to consistency of soft custard by stirring, then whipping if necessary. Add vanilla and whipped cream. Mash or blend peaches with lemon juice. Mix everything together, taste, and add a tablespoon of sugar if necessary, then pour into a refrigerator ice tray and place in freezer until mushy and/or half frozen. Beat again while still soft, then freeze a few hours, until firm.

SERVES 6–10

PEARS

A pear is one of the tenderest and most dependably sweet of all fruits. Don't peel—just wash and eat.

Buy them very hard, and they will ripen beautifully at home. Refrigeration will slow down the ripening process, but, once ripe, they must be eaten promptly, or they will become mushy. Be sure to distinguish between green pears that will turn yellow when ripe and pears that are already ripe when green. If in doubt, ask the produce man.

PEARS IN BRANDIED CHOCOLATE SAUCE

4 pears, peeled and sliced
¼ cup chocolate sauce
few drops brandy

Chill pears and flat-bottomed sherbet cups before you slice and serve. Put slices in sherbet cups, drizzle sauce on top of pears, and a bit of brandy on top of that. Top with little mint leaves dipped in powdered sugar or candied violets (optional).

SERVES 4

PEARS AND GOURMANDAISE CHEESE

Gourmandaise is one of the soft cheeses that are good with most fruits, and notably with pears.

4 pears
8 ounces plain Gourmandaise cheese

Give each person a small knife.

SERVES 4

PEARS AND CAMEMBERT

One of the all-time popular fruit-and-cheese desserts. Nice served with a little brandy or a dessert wine on special evenings.

4 pears
8 ounces Camembert cheese

SERVES 4

PINEAPPLE

This divinely refreshing fruit needs little introduction. Astonishing to look at with its wild brown "eyes" and crown of leaves, it's used as a bowl and a table decoration as well as for just plain eating.

Heavily protected within their bristly skins, most are delicious. For the freshest fruit, avoid sagging frond-tops and moldy bottoms.

PINEAPPLE: A SWEET LIFE
Full of the beautiful sorts of nutrients you'd expect from a land as rich as Hawaii, pineapples literally bristle with natural sugar. They range from tart-sweet to very sweet to incredibly sweet. When they're very sweet, just eat—you can't improve on nature. When tart-sweet, dip in powdered sugar or sweetened whipped cream, or try this:

1 pineapple
1 bowl sweetened whipped cream

Using a sharp knife, cut off top fronds and quarter pineapple. Lie quarters on side and slice away skin. Cut into sticks or wedges. Heap on plate and eat, topped with cream. Pineapple is good chilled and at room temperature. I prefer the latter. It is especially good with strawberries and/or kirsch.

SERVES 3–6

PINEAPPLE CROISSANTS

An astonishingly dramatic-looking creation, pineapple croissants are simply quartered pineapples that are cut ingeniously to look beautiful. They are also beautifully easy to eat. This dish is extremely popular with children, and is known in our family as pineapple boats.

Use a serrated knife with a slight curve, so you can cut along between the pineapple and its rim. If you have a regular straight serrated knife, you can still do it, but the cut won't be as graceful.

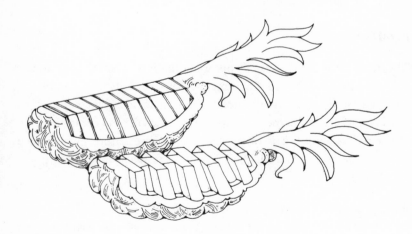

1 pineapple
platter or wooden board
sprinkling of kirsch (for adults)
½ cup powdered sugar in a bowl for dipping

Quarter the pineapple lengthwise, cutting right through the leaves at the top, so that each quarter has its own spike-leafed top. Approach each quarter from the side with your knife and cut a thin rim away from the top. Then cut between pineapple quarter and its skin, as close to the skin as possible (if you're too close the knife will stick). When you've finished, the whole pineapple quarter will be loosened from its shell but still resting there. Now make even crosswise slices, about ¼"–⅓" wide, cutting down into but not through the skin. The pineapple quarter is still resting in its shell. Finally, jog the slices alternately, so that they form a pretty pattern. Each alternate jog should push the pineapple slice about ½" away from the pineapple. Serve the pineapple croissants sprinkled with kirsch if you like. Pass the bowl of powdered sugar.

SERVES 4–6

Variation: In season, small strawberries can be tucked between slices for a more elaborate display.

POMEGRANATES

This fascinating Biblical fruit appears in the fall, when the leaves turn red, and lasts through the Christmas season, when its brilliant, blazing red inner seeds shine like holiday lights in salads, fruit cups, at the breakfast table, and in the most opulent fruit salads and compotes.

Except for jellies, it is rarely cooked, because nature gives it to us perfectly prepared. The tougher the skin, the juicier and more plump the seeds inside.

THE NAKED, BEAUTIFUL POMEGRANATE
The most perfect way to eat a pomegranate is just as nature presents it. Bite into the skin a little to tear it open, then peel the tough skin away with your fingertips. Bit by bit you'll reveal a bounty of glisten-

ing little juicy red ovals. You can pick these away with your fingertips in groups of two or three or six, and pop them into your mouth. When you bite down, the little berries burst into juicy pomegranate flavor, tart enough to tingle, but sweet enough so that sugar is never necessary. These juicy seeds are called pips. The inner structure that holds the seeds is thrown away, like an apple core. If for some reason your pomegranate is stubborn, and you can't pull the seeds away with your fingers, then just bite them away with your teeth (somewhat like eating an ear of corn).

POMEGRANATES FOR DESSERT

Serve a pomegranate on each plate, with a fruit knife, fork, and spoon. (The spoon comes in handy for prying seeds away.) Add a soft dessert-cheese triangle and a biscuit cracker to each plate.

POMEGRANATE PYRAMID

In Israel, this very dramatic salad is displayed during the Succoth holiday. You might also try it at a buffet or luncheon, or when friends come over for dessert and wine.

2 grapefruit, peeled and sectioned
3 tangerines or oranges, peeled and sectioned
seeds of 1 pomegranate

juice of 1 lemon
2–3 tablespoons honey
1 avocado

Make a ring of fanned-out grapefruit sections at bottom of platter. Top with ring of orange sections. (This can be prepared early and kept in refrigerator with plastic wrap on top.) Seed pomegranate and refrigerate. Mix lemon juice and honey and put to one side. Shortly before serving, cut and cube the avocado and put on top of oranges, then sprinkle with pomegranate seeds. Drizzle over all with lemon juice and honey just before serving. Bring to table and dish out individually.

SERVES 6–8

A Child's Garden of Pomegranates

Children are never happier than when they're pulling something apart or eating something sweet. This makes the pomegranate the perfect toy-food. Pomegranates keep for an astonishingly long time in your fruit bowl. They're trusty and portable in school lunches (cut one in half and put in plastic bag). They are sweet elegance eaten by firelight on a chilly fall night. And a TV snack without regrets.

If you live in a warm climate, plant a pomegranate tree. It is stunningly ornamental!

PRUNES

Forget about the digestive virtues of prunes (although it's all true). What they really are is the princess of snacks: candy without guilt.

Prunes in Baggies to go

Into school lunches, out on picnics, in cars, in handbags, at the TV set, at movies, ready in the refrigerator for everyone who's on the run. They're *instant* energy, with lots of sugar built in.

LEMON-PLUMPED PRUNES FOR BREAKFAST

½ pound prunes
juice of 1 lemon
water to cover

Let soak overnight or until prunes are plumped.

Prune Whip

Soak a few prunes in water overnight. Remove pits. Whirl in blender. Fold into a bowl of sweetened whipped cream. Add a squeeze of lemon and sugar if you like.

TANGERINES AND TANGELOS

Ah, heaven. The peels just sort of float off, as though they were waiting for the touch of your fingers.

Tangerines are sweet, tender, and neat to eat. Since they're child's
play to peel, children love them.

SHOPPING FOR TANGERINES
Buy one and peel out a slice. If you've hit on the wildly sweet kind,
then it's time to go on a tangerine binge. Tarter fruit can be dipped in
sweetened whipped cream or powdered sugar.

TANGERINES BY CANDLELIGHT
Serve them by candlelight for dessert, with your favorite exotic
cheeses or simply Gruyère. Think of tangerines as a dressy, formal
fruit. Even the most fumble-fingered guest can cope without spattering,
and ladies with long, dramatic fingernails will not endanger them.

HONEY

Honey is a truly magical food. It is created by bees, from the nectar
and pollen they extract from a whole world of flowers and plants and
blossoming trees. In the process, the honey is pre-digested, and transformed through enzyme activity by the bees into the perfect golden
sweet natural syrup that tastes so good.

Once the bees have completed their honey-making, it is ready to eat.
Since it is pre-digested, it is a natural form of sweet that digests very
easily, and very *quickly*. Athletes love honey, because its gives them
incredibly fast energy with little strain on their systems. Some health
regimens include a tablespoon of honey in a little vinegar on rising
(after you make it through *that* you could probably face anything!)
Divers and cold-weather types often swear by honey, partially for its
warm and instant energy and easy digestion. Sir Edmund Hilary, the
man famous for conquering Mount Everest, was a New Zealand bee-
keeper who grew up on honey instead of sugar. Many singers will not

step on stage without drinking honey in water or milk if their voices are strained, for it soothes their throats.

HONEY, AND HOW TO SHOP FOR AND STORE IT

You should preferably buy raw, unstrained natural honey for the finest flavor and for the best nutrition. Honey does not need to be clarified or heated or have corn syrup added. Check the label to make sure it has not been tampered with. Since natural honey will not spoil in any way, no preservatives are necessary.

Honey is also awesomely stable. It needs no refrigeration and keeps indefinitely. Should it turn a bit granular and sugary with time and certain temperatures, you have only to set it in a pan of hot water, and it will return to silky syrupy smoothness.

Each honey has its own flavor, some are milder, some heartier. Experiment with some of these varieties: tupelo honey from the South, clover honey (a popular favorite), white Dutch clover honey from Louisiana, wild buckwheat honey from California, sage honey, strong and sweet, alfalfa honey, avocado honey, fireweed honey from Washington, wildflower honey, orange blossom honey from Illinois, horse mint honey from Texas, buckwheat honey from New York, sweet clover honey from Wisconsin, blossom honey from flowers of Hawaii, and desertflower honey from California, plus myriad honeys from every state, and surely some special ones from your own region, many hand-bottled at local farms. And others imported from Europe. Try them!

SAVING MONEY WITH HONEY

Since honey keeps indefinitely, you can safely buy it in larger quantities. Two- and 5-pound cans are usually good money-savers. Grade B honey is just as delicious as Grade A.

NAKED, BEAUTIFUL HONEY IN A SUGAR BOWL

The simplest way to use honey is to use it like sugar. Keep it in a sugar bowl or preserves dish right on the breakfast table or nearby, with a spoon and a cover. If it becomes too thick, set in a pan of hot water an inch deep for a few minutes. Use it exactly like sugar, drizzled on cereal, stirred into tea (too rich for coffee), on grapefruit and other fruits. Lovely dripped onto toast and muffins and rolls, or slathered on waffles and pancakes.

HONEY ON YOGURT

The classic way to enjoy both honey and yogurt.

> *1 8-ounce container plain yogurt (or your own homemade)*
> *1–2 tablespoons honey*

Put yogurt into dish, or leave in container, and top with honey. There are two schools of thought on eating it: either you dip into the yogurt and honey each time, so you taste both flavors, or you stir the honey very well into the yogurt, blending flavors together. This makes a heavenly instant breakfast or lunch, and a richly appealing dessert.

GRANDPA'S BANANA-HONEY SHAKE
(See Index)

PAPAYA-HONEY SHAKE
(See Index)

CAKES AND AN ICE

RICH AND EASY CHEESECAKE

1 egg, separated
2 8-ounce packages cream cheese
½ cup sweet condensed milk
¼ teaspoon salt
*¼ teaspoon grated orange or
    lemon rind*

½ teaspoon vanilla
1½ teaspoons gelatin powder
4 tablespoons water
1 tablespoon or more sugar

GRAHAM CRACKER SHELL

¼ cup butter
1½ cups graham cracker crumbs

Beat egg white until stiff. Beat cream cheese with electric beater until fluffy. And egg yolk, milk, salt, citrus rind, and vanilla. Soften gelatin in warm water, or dissolve over hot water. Stir gelatin into cream-cheese mixture. Fold egg white in gently.

Soften butter. Mix with fingers into graham cracker crumbs. Press into pie pan, shaping into crust. Chill until butter firms before pouring in cheesecake mixture. Chill or freeze.

SERVES 8

STRAWBERRY CHEESECAKE

The cheesecake above is good served with crushed, sweetened strawberries on top. Let sugar and berries sit for at least 2 hours to blend flavors.

HALF A TRIFLE

8 ladyfingers (or 8 slices poundcake)
madeira wine (or sherry)
1½–2 cups cut-up fruit (strawberries and peaches)
½ pint heavy cream, sweetened and whipped

Line bottom of four flat-bottomed sherbet cups (or a bowl) with ladyfingers. Sprinkle on wine. Top with cut-up fruit and smother fruit with whipped cream. Garnish top with a few strawberries, cookie crumbs, or the like.

SERVES 4

BISCUIT TORTONI

Biscuit Tortoni was supposedly served first in 1789 in a café in Paris, yet the masters of the ultimate Biscuit Tortoni were the Neapolitan ice cream makers. No matter its true parentage, it's a lovely dessert, and easily frozen, so it might be wise to make an extra amount for the freezer.

1 cup crumbled macaroons   *pinch salt*
2½ cups heavy cream   *1½ teaspoons vanilla extract*
⅓ cup confectioners' sugar   *6–8 pleated paper cups*

Soak macaroons in 1¼ cups cream with sugar and salt until soft and soaked. Whip remaining cream till thick but not stiff. Fold in macaroon mixture and flavor with vanilla. Freeze in pleated paper cups. When frozen, sprinkle with crumbled pralines, toasted chopped almonds, or candied cherry halves. Or anything sweet and sprinkly. Crumbled sweet granola might be a nice contemporary touch.

SERVES 6–8

9. EGGS, MILK, AND CULTURED-MILK PRODUCTS

EGGS

The classic, bravura way to eat raw eggs is to beat them gently with a fork in a glass, then down them, *tout seule,* just like that. Frankly, it takes motivation, or rather it takes quite a bit of doing if you haven't done it before, but it *is* done in the more vital eating circles. Not for the typical brunch. Try it on a few of your more adventurous friends.

> *1 egg (or more)*
> *dash Worcestershire sauce (optional)*

THE CLASSIC EGGNOG

This English classic, like Dickens, only improves when revisited. Splashed with rum, it shows up on holidays, but it really reigns in all its simple glory without alcohol, at breakfast, and often late in the morning after a particularly lengthy night before. And it's a graceful way to win the eat-your-eggs battle with some children.

4 eggs (8 for a sinfully rich eggnog)   *3½ cups milk*
1–2 tablespoons sugar   *nutmeg (optional)*
1 teaspoon vanilla

Put eggs, sugar, and vanilla in blender and whirl for a few seconds. Add milk. Blend for 1 minute, until foam rises about 1″. Pour and serve at once, tasting first to see if a dash more sweetening is needed.

SERVES 4

Eggnogs can of course be made with cream, but these are very rich and calorie-laden and should be saved for special occasions.

THE NAKED, BEAUTIFUL ORANGE NOG

4 eggs
1 teaspoon vanilla
1 tablespoon sugar or honey
3¼ cups orange juice, freshly squeezed or frozen

Blend all in blender, and watch it foam up delightfully. This is an instant breakfast, a summer quencher, an evening cooler. Add ice to blender (2 or 3 cubes) if you want it very, very cold.

SERVES 4

THE PLUSH ORANGE NOG

For special occasions, follow the orange nog recipe above, and then add a dash of lime and a grating or sprinkle of nutmeg. Serve over ice in tall glasses with a slice of lime wedged on rim of glass and green straws. Or add a jigger of whiskey for each person served, and you have a formidable drink.

ASSORTED FRUIT NOGS

The orange nog is listed because eggs and orange juice have such a delicious affinity for each other. But you can toss eggs in with an endless variety of juices in the blender (or by using an eggbeater). Quick breakfasts, now an institution, have become as individual as the persons whipping them up. Some add to their egg, juice and/or milk, their favorite protein powders, special energy builders like brewer's yeast. Some are creative mixes of fruit juices like cranberry/apple/ grape and so on. Some add special mixes from health-food stores, with a dash of honey. Or cherry syrup. Or a banana. Or vanilla. Experiment with what's at hand.

CERTIFIED RAW MILK AND DAIRY PRODUCTS

Until the last century, improper handling of milk sometimes caused a cattle disease called brucellosis to be transmitted as undulant fever in humans. Then Louis Pasteur discovered the cause and source of undulant fever, and evolved a solution to the problem: pasteurization.

Pasteurization is the process we use today, in which, to put it simply, milk is heated and disease-causing bacteria are killed. We all enjoy pasteurized milk products and all are clean and safe, thanks to this process that permits the mass distribution of incredibly large amounts of dairy products at prices all can afford. Raw milk still exists, though, and it is not only delicious, but it contains a group of enzymes and some nutrients that the heat of pasteurization destroys. Today's raw milk is certified, under the control and meeting the rigid standards of the American Association of Medical Milk Commissions, and is safe to drink.

Because more precautions are necessary, raw-milk products cost more, but they are generally dairy foods of very high quality, and have the most impeccable of eating-in-the-raw flavor. If you have certified raw milk available at a dairy in your area, you might sample some natural raw cheeses and butter. The milk products taste almost exactly like pasteurized milk. Here are some of the products offered by a fine California raw-milk dairy:

certified raw milk	*natural Swiss cheese*
certified raw nonfat milk	*raw butter from certified cream*
certified all-purpose raw cream	*golden honey ice cream*
raw buttermilk	*strawberry kefir*
natural mild cheddar cheese	*peach kefir, other kefir flavors*

Raw-milk and pasteurized-milk products are used just the same way in recipes and cooking.

THE CULTURED MILKS

In the good old days, culturing milk was a precious means of "preserving" milk past its natural freshness, a lifesaver when there was no refrigeration. And nature, with its customary wisdom, made these milk products taste good. (So good, in fact, that some prefer them to fresh milk.) Raw milk and cream, left standing, "soured" appealingly. Milk churned into butter left a refreshing liquid that was christened buttermilk. And when various bacterial cultures were introduced (very beneficial and desirable bacteria, we hasten to add), the result was a tangy creamy product: yogurt, kefir, and the tarter acidophilus milk.

Today, cultured milks and byproducts are experiencing a tremendous wave of success that is completely deserved. They are delicious ingredients in an infinite number of recipes, raw and cooked. No pancake could possibly compete with the feather-light joy of a buttermilk pancake. And the renown of such simple yet sumptuous desserts as fresh fruit with yogurt and honey and nuts has spread far and wide.

In addition, all the cultured milks offer a double health attraction. First, they are, like any milk product, outstandingly nutritious. Second, and to some people very important, the culture qualities in these milks do marvelous things for your entire digestive system. All are regularly turned to not only for good taste, but also for maintaining good digestion, and restoring it.

The restoration is sometimes so effective that cultured-milk converts such as yogurt-eaters are fervent enthusiasts who relentlessly recruit new yogurt-eaters, and so on. And tales of the virtues of acidophilus milks range from the modestly ecstatic to the frankly incredible, involving stories of yogurt-eating, vibrantly virile Armenians of 102 and case histories of twitching, dissipated wrecks who are transformed into glowing Adonises by nipping daily at yogurt or acidophilus drinks. Nobody but nobody dares or wishes to disapprove.

The return of these milks is a cultural event to be welcomed.

YOGURT

Yogurt has been around as long as cows have. Once you become accustomed to its tang, it tastes great. If you have problems with that, mix it with sour cream or with honey. Buy it or make your own. It keeps beautifully in the refrigerator, much longer than fresh milk. It's the ideal instant meal.

FLAVORED YOGURT
Fruit flavored yogurt is now a national institution. It tastes wonderful. It's a complete, portable, take-anywhere meal. It is so nutritious and filling that it makes a terrific low-calorie breakfast or lunch. It is a lazy school lunch that any mother can be proud of. It is the best kind of snack food.

FRUIT-ON-THE-BOTTOM YOGURT
Punch a hole in the bottom of the container and upending quickly, so that the fruit syrup spills attractively over the yogurt.

YOGURT FOR BABIES
Babyhood is the best time of all to acquire a fondness for yogurt. Babies like it right away, tanginess and all, because they are born with an instinct for the milk products that are so vital to their growth. Until they're six or eight months old, babies should have only a few teaspoons of yogurt at a time, assuming they are enjoying regular milk products. From eight months on, anything yogurt goes. Yogurt, since it clings to the spoon, tends to help babies when they're first trying to feed themselves. I have fond memories of an eighteen-month-old eating his first lime yogurt with a small spoon. He was hopelessly inefficient with the spoon, and plastered lime yogurt on his forehead and cheeks as often as in his mouth. But he was shrieking with delight. He loved the yogurt, and he knew very well that he was eating it all by himself and really accomplishing something.

YOGURT WITH HONEY

The traditional and all-time-favorite way to eat yogurt sweetly.

> *1 cup yogurt*
> *1 tablespoon or more honey*
> *fresh fruit (optional)*

Heap yogurt in dessert cup or bowl, on top of fruit if used. Drizzle honey on top. Stir honey into yogurt as you're eating it. Sprinkle some granola on top for a change.

SERVES 1

INDEX

and Snow Pea Salad, 136
Stuffed Caps, 132
Stuffed with Oysters, 88
Walnut-Stuffed Mushroom Caps, 132
Wild edible, 131
Mustard Dressing, 79–81

Niçoise, Salade, 91–92
Norimaki Sushi, 78
Nuts, 52–53
  with Brussels Sprouts, 113
  Chestnuts, Celery, and Mushrooms with Onion Dip, 56
  Chestnut Salad, 56
  as dinner, 100–101
  with Fruits, 165
  Fruit-Cheese-Nut Centerpiece Dessert, 168
  Hot Seasoned Pumpkin Seeds, 54
  Peanut Butter, 52–53
  Roll à la 1920, 101–102
  storage of, 101
  Sweet and Nutty Salad with Poppy-Seed Dressing, 102
  Sweet and Nutty Snacks Mix, 55
  Walnut-Stuffed Mushroom Caps, 132
  in Watercress and Turkey Salad, 158

Onion:
  Cucumber, and Tomato Buffet, 29–30
  Marinated, 138
  Zucchini, and Tomato, Marinated, 145
Oranges, 195
  Nog, 213

and Papaya Whip, 198
à la The Ritz Madrid, 196
Sherried Ambrosia, 196–197
Overripe Peach Ice Cream, 200–201
Oxalic acid, 11, 151
Oysters, 84–85
  and Caviar, Venetian Style, 88
  Cocktail in Tomato Cups, 39–40
  on the Half Shell, 86–87
  harvesting of, 85–86
  how to select, 86
  in Mushroom Caps, 88

Pale Wine, Pale Cheese, Pale Fruits (A Country Feast), 30–31
Papayas, 197
  Banana, and Honey Shake, 198
  and Orange Whip, 198
  Seeds, 198
  Slices, Dinner Accompaniment, 198
Parsley, 133
  Butter, 134
  clearing garlic odor with, 134
  with Roquefort or Blue Cheese Dip, 134
  selection and storage of, 133
Peaches, 199
  Dessert Soup with Fresh Berries, 199–200
  Ice Cream, 200–201
  Pie, 200–201
  Shakes, 200
Peanut Butter, Homemade, 52–53
Peanuts:
  with Coleslaw, 115
  and Mixed Cabbage and Cheese Salad, 95